Alive in the Five

The Steelers' 1992 premiership charge

Glen Humphries

ISBN: 978-0-6489911-5-1

Alive in the Five: The Steelers: 1992 premiership charge is copyright Glen Humphries 2023

For more information email dragstermag@hotmail.com. If you loved this book so much that you want to buy some more copies then head over to my micropublishing site Last Day of School (find it at www.lastdayofschool.net). And maybe buy some copies of my other books. They're good, I promise you. And all so reasonably priced.

This book is copyright. All rights reserved. Except for private study, research, criticism or reviews, as permitted under the Copyright Act, no part of this book may be reproduced, stored in a retrieval system, or transmitted in any form or by any means without prior written permission. That's not too much to ask, is it? Though I guess you don't need to be told that. If you're so interested in this book that you've gone to the trouble of reading the fine print on the copyright page, I'm sure you'll do the right thing.

About the Author

Glen Humphries has been a journalist for a long, long time. Since 1994, in fact. He only stumbled into the trade, actually. He wanted to be a dentist or a doctor because he figured they made heaps of cash, but his life course was changed when he did a week's work experience at a local newspaper in Year 11. After that he went to uni in Wollongong and then pestered the *Illawarra Mercury* until they relented and gave him a job. Because an 'about the author' section is the place where you're supposed to say things like this – to make it sound like he knows what the hell he's doing – he has won several awards for writing. One of his books, *The Slab*, was the national winner in the Gourmand World Food Awards. He's been writing and self-publishing books since 2017. You can find them all at his site Last Day of School (lastdayofschool.net). He's also the author of a book about rugby league fights called *Biff*, which is published by Gelding Street Press, a follow-up footy book – *Jack Gibson's Fur Coat* – and a cricket book called *Sticky Wickets*. They're all available in bookstores. He knows this because, every time he goes to one, he checks the sports section just to admire his books on the shelf. Sometimes he even takes photos of it. He only played a few seasons of footy himself in primary school,. For the first season he played on the wing. Not because he was fast (he wasn't) but because the coach figured that's where you put crap players. In Years 5 and 6 a new coach thought he'd go better as lock – which made more sense too because he's never been a little guy. A Dragons fan since he was six years old, he adopted the Steelers as his second favourite team after moving to Wollongong to attend university. So that means the 1999 merger of those two teams was perfect for him. And he is well aware he is likely the only person who feels that way. Still, he feels sorry for Steelers fans, because they were dudded in the merger. Really, every year the team should have an alternate strip that resembles the Steelers jerseys of old. Post-merger, he had a season ticket to games at WIN Stadium for a number of years, until the club jacked up the price while cutting back on the games. Besides, he figured it was better to watch games at home on the lounge; the beer is cheaper and there's never a queue for the toilets. If you've read this far, congratulations. I reckon almost nobody does. If you have get in touch via email or social media with the secret phrase "scooter party". It will be our little joke.

Also by Glen Humphries and published by Last Day of School (www.lastdayofschool.net) unless otherwise noted

Biff: Rugby League's Infamous Fights (published by Gelding Street Press)
Jack Gibson's Fur Coat: Rugby League Oddities and Artefacts (Gelding Street Press)
Sticky Wickets: Australian Cricket's Controversies and Curiosities (Gelding Street Press)
Friday Night at the Oxford
Healer: The Rise, Fall and Return of Tumbleweed
Lull City: The Wollongong Music Scene 1955-2020
The Slab: 24 Stories of Beer in Australia
James Squire: The Biography
Sounds Like an Ending: Midnight Oil, 10-1 and Red Sails in the Sunset
Alright!: Queen at Live Aid
Little Darling: Daryl Braithwaite and The Horses
The Six-Pack: Stories from the World of Beer
Beer is Fun
Night Terrors: The True Story of the Kingsgrove Slasher

To those Steelers fans who still love their team long after they disappeared. I hope this book brings back some good memories of a special season.

Alive in the Five

Introduction

At the end of the 1989 season, Illawarra Steelers fans were at their lowest ebb. They'd just lived through their team's worst season, spending winter weekends at the Wollongong Showground losing week after week. The team had already collected two wooden spoons since debuting in the 1982 season – in 1985 and 1986. The next two years were marginally better – third last in 1987 and 13th out of 16 teams in 1988.

But the 1989 Steelers really stunk up the joint. They won just two games all season – close wins over Manly and St George. And there were some shellackings in that season too. A 48-6 loss in a round five clash against Easts. A week later they went down 44-6 at the hands of Canberra. The last round, Cronulla tore them up to the tune of 46-14. A surprise run in the midweek National Panasonic Cup took a little of the sting out of what would be the Steelers' worst season ever.

Yet no-one was expecting where the Steelers would be in just three short years …. Alive in the five.

1

It only took two years after the Sydney league competition launched with nine teams for the sport to get a start in the Illawarra. In 1910, the Illawarra league was born at what was then the Terminus Hotel next to Wollongong station. In that first year, three fledgling clubs played friendlies against each other, before a real competition kicked off in 1911 with teams from Dapto, Unanderra, Mt Keira, Helensburgh and Wollongong.

For the first 60-odd years, the league was strong in the Illawarra; grandstands were full for the grand finals, local media gave over a chunk of their sports pages to cover the games. That other league competition happening just up the road in Sydney didn't really matter – well, most of the time.

Every now and then, thoughts would stray up the road, wondering how an Illawarra team would handle the Sydney competition. That usually happened when the locals managed to knock off a visiting team, giving Illawarra a measure of how they stacked up against the rest of the league world.

One of those moments happened in late August 1931

when minor premiers Balmain played a Group 7 rep team (oddly, it was a match played in the week between the Sydney semi and final). The locals won 19-18, though the *Mercury* may have overstated things a tad by saying the victory shocked the entire state.

"Many games have been judged as the greatest ever, but Group 7's victory will long live in the memory of those fortunate enough to witness the battle," the *Mercury* reported.

At half-time the rep team had seemed overwhelmed by the Sydney visitors, going into the sheds down 18-6. Those in the stands figured the game was as good as over. But the coach must have had some choice words to say in the sheds, because a different rep side came out for the second half.

"Upon resumption it was readily perceived that Balmain were going to get more than bargained for," the *Mercury*'s match report stated. "Gone was the local inferiority complex so pronounced in the first half. Reputations were forgotten, vicious tackles spoilt the cohesion of the Balmain backline."

The Group 7 side ran in three second-half tries while managing to keep the Tigers scoreless. Balmain had a chance to snatch victory at the death; with the scoreboard reading 19-18, the Tigers' Bill Johnson attempted a penalty goal that looked like it was going straight between the posts, only to dip and hit the crossbar.

A week later Balmain flogged Souths in the Sydney premiership decider to the tune of 33-4. Understandably, that made the locals think the talent in the Illawarra could match it with the best in the state.

A year after the end of World War II, they got the chance to stand up against an international side. The British Lions came to Australia to contest The Ashes. As was the tradition at the time, the visitors also played a host of other fixture against country rep sides (all-up the Lions played 20 games in a month).

On June 2, the Brits played a South Coast rep team at the Wollongong Showground, a day after the visitors had defeated a NSW side 14-10. The Illawarra side knocked over the Lions 15-12.

"From the kick-off they did not allow reputations to worry them and their tackling was so severe that the Englishmen were not able to settle down," the *Mercury* reported. "The visitors tried every trick they knew but the locals did not hang off them or take dummies as the New South Welshmen had done the previous day."

The locals saw this as evidence of the robust health of their league, noting the Lions would only lose two other times on the tour (to Newcastle and Queensland). What they overlooked was that the Brits finished the game with 11 men due to injury. One left the field minutes into the second half, a second 10 minutes later and a third shortly before the final siren. Also, seven of the players had taken the field against NSW a day earlier.

"When I saw the Englishmen in rooms at a hotel in Wollongong after yesterday's match," reported the *Sydney Morning Herald*'s Tom Goodman, "the scene resembled that of a casualty clearing station."

At any rate, the win started people thinking about entering a team in the Sydney competition. Among those were officials from the Port Kembla club, the side that had appeared in every grand final from 1941-1946, winning five of them. But with the Sydney league having already accepted Manly and Parramatta's bids for the 1947 season, there was little chance of Port Kembla being successful. Incidentally, the Blacks would continue their purple patch, appearing in the next four grand finals (for the record, between 1940 and 1950, they only missed one decider).

As any Illawarra footy fan knows, the Sydney clubs had never been averse to poaching local talent for the big league. Players like Graeme Langlands, Keith Barnes, Garry Jack, Bob Fulton, Steve Morris, Steve Roach and Craig Young all started out playing for Illawarra clubs before Sydney team swooped and took them away.

Usually the player movement was all one-way traffic, until one very ambitious Illawarra official decided to turn the tables.

2

Illawarra Leagues Club secretary Dudley Locke hatched an audacious scheme to poach at least eight top-flight players from the Sydney competition and send one to each local team. The plan was bankrolled by the large funds from the leagues club, which had officially opened in 1951. Two years later, in part because of the large amounts of beer being sold at the club (it went from 74 gallons a week when the club opened to 720 gallons in 1953), Locke had enough ready cash to spend £12,500 on buying players. He refuted the suggestion that the club was "angling" to get an Illawarra team into the Sydney competition. "That's ridiculous," Locke said. "We will make our competition so strong down here that Sydney clubs will want to play in it."

On June 10, 1953, a touring US team played a country side at Wollongong Showground. The match saw an influx of Australian players, where the leagues club started secret negotiations with some of them. Once word got out that the club was waving around lucrative contracts there was interest from a lot of players, the *Sydney Morning Herald* reported.

By this stage, the media had linked one very big player to

the Illawarra Leagues Club bid – Kangaroo captain and South Sydney player Clive Churchill. The gossip was that he had already signed a five-year deal to play in Wollongong from 1954. Both Locke and Churchill tried to scotch the rumours. "There has been talk of my transferring there," Churchill told the Sydney press, "but my home is here and I would not do anything before seeing South Sydney."

A few days later, Locke let the cat out of the bag while announcing he had signed Country winger Jack Lumsden and Kangaroo centre Harry Wells. "The Illawarra club is trying to engage a number of topline players," he said. "We are trying to form a strong competition here. We have made overtures to other players, including Clive Churchill, but as yet only two have been signed."

That was enough to put the wind up South Sydney, who went to a meeting of the NSW League and tabled a motion specifically designed to halt Locke's plan. The club wanted to see all players in the Kangaroo team soon to tour New Zealand bound to their present club for the next season. Which would obviously mean Souths would get to keep Churchill. It was narrowly defeated 18-14.

On the weekend of June 20, Churchill travelled down to Wollongong to sign a £2500 contract that would see him play in the Illawarra league for five seasons; the leagues club also committed to finding him a house and a job. "An offer like mine was too good to reject," Churchill said. "Sydney clubs could not give me anything like the terms, so when I saw that there was good accommodation and a steady job I snapped up the offer."

Among the other players who took advantage of the

leagues club's cash splash were Noel Pidding, Brian Carlson, Brian Orrock and Churchill's Souths team-mate Les Cowie. In Sydney, footy teams decided there was some merit in this unique funding model and decided to set up their own leagues clubs.

"Most Sydney clubs realise that the only counter to the Wollongong plan is cash," the *Sunday Mail* reported, "and that it can be made in large enough amounts only by clubs along the Illawarra lines.

"St George has already established its 'social club'. Canterbury-Bankstown will have one going before next season. South Sydney and Manly-Warringah have ideas, and this week a supporter offered North Sydney £1000 to get its club started. If they get enough liquor licences they'll be right."

When the Illawarra Leagues Club allocated the players to various clubs in the Wollongong competition; Christian Brothers (now Collegians) got the prize of Churchill for the 1954 season. The leagues club also offloaded to the clubs the responsibility of fulfilling the promise of a house and a job for each player. The clubs had 60 days to take care of that, otherwise the leagues club would step in and reallocate the players.

But The Little Master was getting cold feet; he found the flat he had been promised was in disrepair and the top-notch role he was supposed to have at the leagues club was behind the bar. But perhaps top of Churchill's mind was that his wife was unhappy about leaving the big smoke. "I signed the contract with the Illawarra Leagues Club in haste," he told the *Sydney Morning Herald*, "and I now regret it. My wife does not want to go to Wollongong."

He was interested in becoming a publican; so Souths aimed to woo him back with the help of supporters willing to help him achieve that goal. "My present plans are to play in Wollongong next year," said Churchill, muddying the waters, "but I also have the chance of moving into the hotel business.

"Should this happen I may retire from football until the business is well-established. This does not mean that I am contemplating retiring from football forever."

Not surprisingly, Locke was most unimpressed. "Churchill is bound to play in Wollongong for the next five years," he said. "He has signed a £2500 contract and has agreed to work at the Illawarra Social Club. We will not release him from his contract." He added he would make sure the Souths player did not play anywhere else for the five-year length of the contract.

The NSW League stepped in to help Souths and Churchill by stating that, as the Illawarra Leagues Club wasn't affiliated with the Sydney body that it would not recognise the contract Locke had devised. Rather conveniently, at the very same meeting, Souths tabled Churchill's freshly-signed contract for registration. Churchill's Souths team-mate Cowie also wanted out of his Wollongong contract.

Locke said he wasn't too concerned with what Cowie did; it was Churchill's reneging and the precedent it was setting he was unhappy with. "We are not in the least concerned about what the NSW Rugby League does in this matter," he said. "Its attitude is consistent with the attitude of all district clubs in Sydney. For years they have pilfered the greatest players the country has had. Clive Churchill is an example.

"We are trying to restore country football to its former strength. But now the League has said Churchill will not play here many of the other players we have signed up are not keen to join us. Churchill is the backbone of the team we are building."

The player regretted what he had done but felt he had made the right move for himself. "I feel sure Wollongong would have released me from the contract if I had explained," he said, and then walked back his complaint of being offered dud employment. "Wollongong was giving me a good job in the leagues club, but I now find I am doing better in Sydney."

In October 1953, he sought permission to speak to the leagues club at its next meeting – and then didn't show. Churchill decided a Thursday night meeting wasn't convenient – which really sounds like the actions of a man not keen to face the music. So his lawyer had to deliver the bad news that Churchill felt the contract he signed with the Illawarra Leagues Club wasn't binding, and he owed it to rugby league to stay with Souths. Oh yeah, and he didn't like the job the club found him either – even though he had days earlier called it a "good job".

"My client also desires that I point out to you that, with respect to the position offered to him," the lawyer said "it would appear that the position offered to my client would entail him working in an unregistered club where the law so far as the Gaming and Betting Act is concerned is constantly broken and, of course, should the police at any time in the future take action, then his security of employment would be greatly jeopardised."

Locke said that was crap; the club had a liquor licence and no gambling was allowed. He was very unimpressed with Churchill indeed – in fact most of the city was. "This joker has captained Australia for 40 matches – an all-time record – and when a chap like that wallows in the dirt something should be done," Locke told the meeting.

"You can be quite sure that had this club fallen down on its side of the contract, there was no doubt what Churchill would have done. I am quite sure he would have demanded and sued us for the £2500 and for the £15 per week guaranteed wage for five years."

So that's the same course of action the leagues club took; they engaged the services of a QC and prepared to drag Churchill through the courts. "Churchill's arrogant attitude has decided us on this action," Locke told the media.

The plan was to restrain him from playing elsewhere and consider claiming damages. There was no expectation that this would be a quick fix; Locke wasn't expecting to see the court case start for months. In the meantime he continued waving money around to drag elite players to the Illawarra.

One of those was Puig Aubert, the best French league player of all time. And perhaps one of the most unusual; the fullback was reputed to have taken a cigarette on the field several times, once catching a ball with one hand because he held a ciggie in the other. Locke offered the Frenchman £14,000, which included a £6250 sign-on fee, £500 per year as a playing bonus and a job with a guaranteed weekly wage of £20.

Locke was also thinking outside the league square, looking to bring top-class soccer player Stanley Matthews over to play his sport locally. He got the same offer as Aubert. NSW Soccer Football Association director JC Cobb thought it a good idea but not enough to entice Matthews to the South Coast. And anyway, it would be better to spread that money around the players already here. "I would like to see a number of such players put on a full-time or part-time coaching basis and told to concentrate on the schoolboys and the junior players," Cobb said. "If this is done, the full effects will not be seen for perhaps five years, but the results will be well worthwhile, even spectacular."

In the end neither sportsman took Locke up on his offer. Meanwhile, the grand scheme to buy a player for each local league team had well and truly come unstuck. Churchill and Cowie had already left, while Ken McCaffrey wasn't keen to play with Western Suburbs and Port Kembla didn't want their allocated player Brian Carlson.

Meanwhile, up in Sydney, Churchill had pulled on the Souths jersey for a few trial matches ahead of the 1954 season; making it perfectly clear he wasn't going to honour his Illawarra contract. After Churchill finally came down to face the committee in March, the leagues club agreed to let both he and Cowie out of their contracts.

Churchill admitted he should have spoken to the club much, much earlier. But, like so many footballers who would come after him, Churchill recognised his time in the game was short and he had to make hay (ie cash) while the sun was shining.

"'I am now recognised as one of Australia's leading footballers, but I have seen some of the world's best today, become a has-been tomorrow – forgotten by those who came to cheer – and left entirely to their own resources," he told the committee. "I hope to play representative football for many years yet but I have an obligation to myself and my family to ensure that when I am forgotten I will have something."

There was no word on whether the leagues club got something in return for stepping aside. Though Locke's efforts did have the effect of creating a resurgence of interest in the local league as people began to pack the grandstands to watch the games.

3

While the Illawarra league was happy to exist for so long entirely separate from Sydney, the two competitions were very much alike. Especially when it came to the rough stuff. Reading through local media coverage of Illawarra matches it's clear things got wild and wooly sometimes. Take this example from the *Mercury* in 1920, where the writer expressed concerns about the unruly crowd at Bode's Oval – which was built near what is now the North Gong Hotel and was, for a time, the premier sporting facility in town.

"...There was only one police officer present, the crowd getting very excited, crowding the playing area. Squabbles and fights in different parts of the ground, and more furious onslaughts around the hotel, naturally one officer could not cope with the demands, though he put forth every effort, and on one occasion was placed in a very ugly situation against big odds, still he stuck to his post.

"Now that the termination of the League competition is drawing to a very interesting stage, and naturally excitement rising to boiling point, the crowds will be more difficult to control, thus necessitating greater and closer supervision.

"It is to be hoped that the league officials will put forth a strenuous effort in the future, to secure more police protection if possible, feeling sure that one man is unable to cope with the demand."

In 1925 the referee called off a match between Bombo and Glebe because players had been threatening to beat him up. "Bombo players played in a rough, unsportsmanlike manner," the *South Coast Times* reported, "and when cautioned threatened him with violence. Barrackers urged Bombo players with such expression as 'put the boot into him', 'punch him' and so on."

Wests and Corrimal fought out a 15-all draw in 1950, with each side having a player sent off. "Corrimal lost their big, bullocking forward McClusky late in the second half when he stood up in a set scrum and clocked Wests' forward Col Longhurst with a terrific punch. Longhurst was KO'd by the blow."

The 1954 final had a strange incident where police detective Jack Hurley and Sergeant Perce Russell entered the Wollongong sheds at half-time and threatened to charge prop Bill Hodges with on-field assault against Port Kembla players. "The police sergeant talks to me at half-time," Hodges told the papers. "He said 'if you go on the way you did in the first half and deliberately maim a footballer, I will go on the field and arrest you and charge you with assault'."

The detective told Hodges's captain Bill Bartlett to order the prop to cut out the rough play, but Bartlett refused. The rest of the team threatened to boycott the match if Hodges was taken to the slammer.

A day later, club officials met with police Inspector JR

Sellwood to discuss the incident. Afterwards the inspector said police action had "a beneficial effect on both teams in the second half" but there were no further steps the law needed to take. Reading between the lines, detective Hurley had overstepped the mark and likely got a bit of a bum-kicking later.

The Wollongong club also decided to let it go as well. But Port Kembla official RJ Nicolas wanted it known the cops had been in *his* team's shed at half-time as well, lest the Wollongong club think someone in the Port Kembla team was "squealing". It also turned out that Hurley may not have been an impartial bystander; his brother Leo was Port Kembla's hooker.

A day later, referee Jack Underwood decided to get involved as well, wanting to scotch rumours that it was he who called the cops. "I consider the police intervention an unjust reflection on my ability as a referee," he said.

Underwood said the police tried to stop him going out for the second half, warning him that he may not finish the game. "I am not out to protect any individual," he said, after lodging a formal protest with the referees association, "but I feel that the whole police intervention was unwarranted."

Underwood also found himself in trouble during a match between Norths and Wollongong at Helensburgh. He had sent off three players and, after full-time, the local crowd chose to show its disapproval by pelting him with rocks. The ref was concerned because the safety of the dressing sheds was several hundred metres away. "I knew I was in trouble and couldn't make it," he said. "So I asked a Norths official for police protection." Turned out there would be none coming as the first player he sent off was the town's policeman.

In 1966, the local league saw fit to suspend Dapto third grader Barry Purdie for a decade after he punched a referee while watching a junior footy match at Corrimal. The board thought the matter so serious they decided to hear the case themselves, rather than take the usual process of leaving it in the hands of the judiciary.

A feisty 1978 semi between Port Kembla and Dapto saw referee Kevin Riolo needing a police escort from the field after giving five players their marching orders in eight minutes.

Wests prop Harry Eden was the first to get marched, in the 30th minute of the first half after Port's captain Peter Fitzgerald was knocked down near the posts. Team-mates Kon Demos and Barry Pearson (playing his 100th match for Wests – he was presented with a silver tea set before the match) were sent off for their involvement in an all-in brawl, as was Port Kembla's Hugh Douglas. The last to go was Wests centre Tim Edwards over a high tackle on Fitzgerald.

When Edwards was marched, Wests players began to walk off the field in protest at being left with nine players for half the match. Only the intervention of coach Tommy Bishop got them back on the field. Not surprisingly, the Wests supporters in the crowd were rather unhappy with Riolo and his touch judges – one spectator threw an unspecified missile at them – and eight police officers had to be called to escort them from the field. Despite having to play with nine men to Port's 12, Wests managed to keep the score close, going down 25-19. The Red Devils actually outscored Port 14-11 in the second half.

At the judiciary a day later all five players were suspended, with Demos and Edwards copping a two-week ban, while the others were outed for a week. That meant Douglas would miss the grand final, which Port qualified for having beaten Wests. Red Devils officials planned to appeal the decision and there was talk of the club boycotting the final against Dapto – in part because Riolo was again the man in the middle.

In reality, the club was never going to boycott the final, but they had other ways to raise the ire of the league. Like naming the suspended players in their team for the match. To justify the move officials said the players had to be included in the team sheet in the event their appeals to be heard later in the week were successful. If they were to wait until the outcome of the appeals, it would be too late to add them to the team if they were exonerated.

Meanwhile, Riolo and the other officials were concerned it would all kick off again in the final and asked for police protection. Pearson and Eden had their suspensions lifted in time for the match, but Bishop admitted the controversy had taken a toll on his players.

"The events of the last week have knocked the boys about quite a bit but I'm certain they'll produce top football against Dapto – no matter what the circumstances," he said.

The minor premiers beat a Dapto side that included Steve Morris playing his last game before moving to the St George Dragons. A week later, Wests ran up against Port Kembla in the grand final, winning 17-13.

Perhaps the strangest incident in the Illawarra

competition was the effort to fix the 1970 grand final between Dapto and Wests. Dapto trainer Les Griffin said representatives of a gambling syndicate approached him first on the way to work and again on his lunch break. Their offer was to pay him to dope Dapto captain-coach Lionel Simmonds, Bob Lanigan and Gwil Barnes.

"I first thought it was some sort of bad joke," Griffin said, "but when I realised the men were serious about the possibility of doping members of my team I told them where to go.

"I have never heard a proposition like it. One of the three men is a pretty tough-looking character and I could not make up my mind what action to take after I had again refused to listen to the offer."

Dapto secretary Wal Brown decided to introduce security measures for the team's last training session and close down the sheds on game day to everyone barring players and officials.

As one of the targets of the doping attempt Simmonds was taking the whole thing very seriously. "My players have been told not to accept drinks from strangers and to be on the alert for drug-laced food and drinks," he said.

"I will tell them to eat and drink at home. And before the match we will go to a Wollongong motel as a final safety precaution."

All the club's safety measures came to nought; Dapto lost the grand final to Wests 12-4. So the mobsters who tried to fix the game were probably happy they got the result they wanted while also saving money.

4

There were several attempts by the Illawarra to join the Sydney competition well before the Steelers' first season in 1982. Around the same time Locke was trying to entice Churchill to Wollongong, the local league decided to call on the NSWRL to bring in two country teams (one of them obviously being Illawarra). It didn't work – the Country Rugby League (CRL) didn't want to damage two strong local competitions for the benefit of Sydney's and several Wollongong clubs weren't fans of the idea either.

The district tried again in 1965 but the CRL again refused to let them go. But through the 1970s, interest in the local league waned; teams folded and crowds started to find other things to do. This was in part a result of the fight by Balmain Tiger Dennis Tutty to overturn the transfer system, where a player was tied to a club – even if they were off-contract – until it wanted to let the player go. If they did agree to let the player leave, their new club would have to pay a transfer fee. With Tutty winning his fight at the end of 1971, the poaching of local talent by Sydney clubs picked up in pace. This obviously led to a weakening of the local league.

As a result of the decline, by the late 1970s the local Illawarra media chose to focus on the Sydney competition. Before then the back pages of the *Mercury* were given over to the Illawarra league every winter.

Construction of the F6 motorway linking Wollongong with southern Sydney and moves to electrify the South Coast line also brought Sydney closer to Wollongong and made the idea of fans of an Illawarra team travelling to away games at Endeavour Oval or Henson Park more realistic.

The opposition to joining the Sydney competition had, therefore, diminished. So, in March 1980, the Illawarra Rugby League (IRL) accepted the NSWRL offer to join a proposed second division competition for the 1981 season. The idea for the new division is that it would operate with the top grade on a promotion and relegation basis. But after coming up with the proposal for a second division, the NSWRL began dithering so, by September 1980, the locals decided time was getting away from them. With a 1981 start unlikely, the IRL threw caution to the wind and voted to enter the top grade – even though they hadn't been invited.

NSWRL boss Kevin Humphreys saw it that way, figuring you don't demand to be included, you wait until you're asked. IRL secretary Bob Millward dug in his heels – it was the top grade or nothing. The cards landed Illawarra's way when the second division concept fell over, leaving the top grade as the only place to put the South Coast team. In a presentation to the NSWRL, the Illawarra bid said it was a case of now or never. "The game in the Illawarra at the standard known in the past and as you know at present will not be available for consideration to a higher competition in three years' time," it stated.

"Gentlemen, the Illawarra Rugby League tried unsuccessfully to enter the Sydney first division in 1954 and 1966. This application is made in different and in fact desperate circumstances. As previously indicated, this will be the last ... the opportunity will not be available in the future with the game's present trend in the Illawarra."

The NSWRL's concerns that the Illawarra's admission as the 13th team would force the need to introduce a bye were forgotten and the league voted 38-4 in favour of the new club for the 1982 season. Canberra would also be admitted, bringing the competition to 14 teams and eliminating any need for a bye.

Nine months before the 1982 season kicked off, the new club unveiled its mascot and logo. After passing on suggestions like Shorthorns, Steelies, Brumbies and Leisure Coasters, they went with Steelers. On June 23, 1981, the *Mercury* unveiled the now-iconic Steelers logo, which it described as "a futuristic man in armour". Over that futuristic man's right shoulder was a part of the logo that would soon disappear – a silhouette of the Port Kembla steelworks, complete with smoke blowing out of the stack. "Illawarra now join Newtown as the only Sydney rugby league teams not to feature an animal in their emblem – a sign of the future," reported the *Illawarra Mercury*.

By mid-1981, work was already under way on finding the estimated $320,000 needed to get the club up and running. Dapto, Collegians, Wollongong, Illawarra, Corrimal, Thirroul and Wests leagues clubs would kick in a total of $120,000 a year, and sponsors including jersey manufacturer

Classic and footwear company Dunlop also signed up.

Part of the argument for admission was that the Illawarra was the oft-cited "rugby league nursery". Plenty of players had started out in the Illawarra league before getting the call-up to the Sydney comp. Perhaps there was the expectation that, with such a nursery to call on, an Illawarra side would be competitive from day one. But the reality was quite different; most of those players who left to sign up with Sydney clubs were never going to come back, and others in the local competition would still choose to sign with clubs other than the Illawarra.

The Steelers did look to former locals and current St George players Brian Johnson and Steve Morris, but to no avail. They did, however, manage to steal a few players from Sydney teams. Fullback, former Kangaroo and one-time teenage star in the local league John Dorahy opted not to re-sign with Manly and ignored interest from St George, Wests, Easts, Newtown, Canberra and even a preferred move to Brisbane to play for Redcliffe to sign with the Steelers and become their inaugural captain.

"Bob Millward's honesty and most of all his lack of pressure completely swung us around," Dorahy remembered. "He didn't get upset with our talks with Brisbane so we didn't conduct an auction with him. All he would say was 'okay, what else can I do to get you to play here?'."

The new club also landed Brian Hetherington and Barry Jensen from the previous season's grand finalists Newtown and Greg Cook from the Bulldogs.

One of the earliest signings wasn't a player but a trainer.

The new club managed to woo Ken Boothroyd down south after working at the Dragons from 1970-77 and Norths from 1979. One of his tactics would be to play disco hits from The Village People, Donna Summer, The Pointer Sisters and Lipps Inc during gym sessions, believing it improved the players' efforts.

In July, the important decision of appointing a coach was made, with former Balmain premiership player Allan Fitzgibbon hired for the job. Fitzgibbon had been coaching over at Dapto since 1971, winning four premierships, so had to tender his resignation to the Canaries.

"It will be a long, hard road… I know that," Fitzgibbon said. "Success won't happen overnight. But it has been proved over a long period that Illawarra can produce players who make the grade in Sydney. My hope is that some of the good young talent here, added to a selection of players from outside, will give us a firm foundation for 1982."

The locals got their first view of the Steelers not at their Wollongong home ground but at Dapto Showground in a February 6 trial against the Rabbitohs. Fitzgibbon treated it like a trial and used a squad of 22 players, while Souths stuck with their strongest 13. That was a large factor in the result – a crowd of just over 8000 watched the Steelers lose 25-5. But Souths coach Bill Anderson found some nice words for the local media. "Have no doubt, the Steelers worried us early," he said. "The Steelers will be a big handful for most teams."

Oddly, one of the key takeaways for the club in this trial was that they might need to put barbed wire around the Wollongong Showground playing surface for Round One.

Dapto Showground – like the Steelers home ground – had a dog track ringing the field. During the trial fans spilled out onto the track; the concern was that in doing so they had covered the advertising around the perimeter. "We'll have to take a long look at the issue after what happened at Dapto," boss Bob Millward said. "We've got to protect the advertisers' rights and we've got to keep the people off the field."

By the time the Steelers first-round match against Penrith came around on February 28, 1982, some action had been taken on fencing. Footage of early games suggest some fencing went up to keep the spectators out.

"At 5pm on Sunday, the Illawarra Steelers clash with the Penrith Panthers in a rugby league match that marks the beginning of a new era in sport in the region," the *Mercury* said on the front page of a souvenir edition.

"It's the start of Illawarra's participation in the greatest rugby league competition in the world, and is the culmination of years of hard work and dedication by many. The club has bought wisely and on Sunday will field a team that the region can be proud of. Success will be hard to come by at first, but we believe Illawarra will emerge as one of the top clubs in a few years."

That first premiership match wasn't a win for the Steelers, going down 17-7 after Penrith set up a 14-0 lead at the break. "The Steelers looked nervous and lacked cohesion in attack," the *Mercury* noted, "but coach Allan Fitzgibbon is confident that will be overcome as the players get used to each other."

There were a few flare-ups in the game, one of which led to Jensen becoming the first Steelers player to be sinbinned.

During the Steelers' attempted comeback late in the game, the soon-to-be-familiar chant of "Steelers ... Steelers ... Steelers" rose up from the 9562-strong crowd. The Steelers had their chances; half Lee Pomfret twice missed grounding a ball in-goal from kicks and other possible tries were denied by the Panthers' strong cover defence.

The *Mercury* coverage noted a lack of any pre-match build-up with the odd sight of the Panthers cheer squad performing in the middle of the Steelers' home ground. "If there was anything missing yesterday (besides a home-town win) it was the complete lack of promotional razzamatazz," the paper reported, adding that the Steelers' jerseys in the crowd were outnumbered by those of various Sydney clubs.

"Steelers officials admit they'll have a hard time winning over the die-hard club supporters but regional pride has a habit of winning in the end," the *Mercury* reported.

"It's hard to sit through a game without getting excited when the bloke next door or the bloke you used to know at school is charging for the line. That's what the Steelers have to offer – the chance to see OUR TEAM taking on the best rugby league teams in the world."

The Steelers' first win came in Round Three in a 20-10 home victory over Souths. The first win was always going to be a bit of a big deal, especially against a team that had scored 67-7 in their first two matches – and the Steelers bouncing back after a 40-15 drubbing a week earlier. But *Mercury* league reporter Charlie Richardson may have overstated thing a bit in his match report.

"The Steelers ripped through the Rabbitohs for four classy tries and a crowd of 6992 fans ignored the rain as the baby club of the NSWRL hurled 75 years of tradition aside and humbled the might of South Sydney," Richardson wrote.

Captain Dorahy, who maintained his perfect goalkicking record of 16 from 16 (including trials) called it the best win of his career. "They don't come any better than that after some of the knocking that we've taken," he said. In his *Mercury* column, coach Fitzgibbon praised his team for the win. "By the way my blokes played the Illawarra fans can get set for plenty more."

But it was a false dawn. The breakthrough win was followed by five straight losses, which put them in last spot come Round Eight. There would only be five more wins that season, one of which would forever remain the Steelers' biggest win. That was a 45-0 throttling of fellow newcomer Canberra at Wollongong (ironically, in front of the Steelers' smallest home ground that season) after leading 17-0 at half-time.

Wingers Lee Pomfret and Peter Kirkland both scored hat-tricks in the nine-try romp. Prop Peter Ryan played the bulk of the game with a broken collarbone he picked up the previous week but had hidden from the Steelers' medical staff. Because of the pain he'd hardly had any sleep for a week; which is why he fell asleep in the car on the way to the game and had to be woken when they got to the showground.

"I wanted to get on that field today and be part of a big win against Canberra," he said. "I didn't let my mates down. All the pain was worthwhile."

A week later, the Steelers came crashing down, creating the unusual feat of racking up the team's all-time biggest loss right after their biggest ever win. The team travelled to Henson Park only to have Newtown wallop them 51-0. "More Jets touched down at Henson Park yesterday than at Kingsford Smith Airport," the *Mercury* reported.

Newtown coach Warren Ryan, who had made the pre-season comment that signing with the Steelers was like booking a ticket on the Titanic, chose to sink the boot in again. "It is quite obvious Steelers manager Bob Millward still has his L plates showing," Ryan said.

An ugly point in the debut season took place in a Round 18 home match against Wests. With the match just 90 seconds old, Wests prop Bob Cooper went wild and whacked three Steelers – Greg Cooper, Lee Pomfret and Scott Greenland. There were rumours a get-square was in the offing; Illawarra players were unhappy with Cooper after a reserve grade incident earlier that year where he was sent off for using his knees on a Steelers player.

Cook went to hospital with a suspected fractured skull, while Pomfret had a fractured nose and a broken jaw. On the following day's front page, the *Mercury* ran a photo of the battered Pomfret, his face smeared with blood.

"The violence that erupted at the start of Sunday's match was a disgrace," editor Peter Newell wrote. "One player is in hospital with a fractured cheekbone, a smashed nose and facial fractures at the base of his nose. Another player went to hospital and has to return there today for treatment for a compound fracture of the nose and a broken upper jaw.

"Punch-ups might be great crowdpullers today. But tomorrow they will be the very reason for the code's death rattle."

The fight effectively ended Cooper's league career. He was sent off and copped a 15-month ban, signing with Norths when he came back but only managing four games. Cook's top-grade career would be over at the end of 1983. As for Pomfret, he would make it back and play 15 games in the 1983 season. But that would be his last year in the top grade as well.

The Steelers lost that match against Wests 23-5, and went on to lose six of their remaining eight games to end up second-last on the ladder, four points clear of wooden spooners Canberra.

5

When the second season rolled around, the Steelers had landed its first jersey sponsor. A three-year sponsorship deal with Penfolds saw the Kaiser Stuhl logo embroidered on the jerseys. The big signing of forward Mark Broadhurst from Manly (perhaps best remembered for the on-field brawl with Newtown's Steve Bowden in the 1981 finals series) and victories in all three trial games raised hopes that 1983 would be better than 1982.

Pomfret made his return to football in one of those trials, against Norths at Dapto Showground. His injury from last season's punch required wiring and a plate in his face. "Norths seemed really aware of the situation," Pomfret said. "They gave us a bit of a test-out. I copped a really good box in the ear at one stage. It probably did me a favour – after that I was right."

Things didn't go too well for the Steelers from the start of the competition. The Steelers opened the season with a six-match losing streak. By Round 10, the team had just a single win; after that point, the season was pretty much over in terms of any finals dreams. They gave the fans something to cheer about late in the season with a run of four wins from five games.

One of those was a tight match against the Bears, won 21-11 via an ugly Broadhurst field goal with just a minute left in the game. "I've always had a burning ambition to kick a field goal," he said, "now it's fulfilled."

Famed runner Cliff Young kicked off the last round match against Penrith at the showground, which was also a farewell for Fitzgibbon, who had announced his decision to step down as coach earlier that week. The Steelers couldn't see him off with a win, going down 26-12. They had improved slightly on the debut season, winning eight games and finishing in 12th spot.

Off the field things were just as tough for the team. The year 1983 brought with it a recession, which was felt harder in Wollongong than most places. It was an era of part-time players, where they all had day jobs. With big employers the mines and the steelworks cutting back, as many as 10 Steelers were out of work at any one time during the season. Darryl Duncan, an off-season purchase, headed back home to Queensland when he couldn't find work.

To add to those woes, several of the local leagues clubs that promised funds in the debut year withdrew their support, costing the club around $80,000 a season. By the end of the season, the club was in deficit to the tune of $220,000.

To try and dig themselves out of a big deficit, the club hit upon the novel idea of staging a rock concert at Brandon Park. Headlined by Australian Crawl, the January 1984 show also featured Moving Pictures, The Sunnyboys, Uncanny X-

Men, The All-Niters and local band Hot Ice. A fair bit of work was needed to get the site ready for the concert – electricity had to be routed in and a sturdy fence built around the area to stop interlopers.

No alcohol was allowed to be brought into the concert; though some clever souls snuck onto the site a week before the concert and buried their booze, while others used the old trick of bringing oranges injected with vodka.

The concert helped the Steelers' bottom line, raising an estimated $50,000 for the club. As well as the cash, the team also needed a new coach. They had their eye on Souths' Bill Anderson; he knocked them back but recommended former assistant Brian Smith, who had been sacked by the Bunnies at the end of the 1982 season. The Steelers offered him the coaching role and he accepted. "It's a great challenge and, while there's a lot of work to be done, I'm confident we'll be a force to be reckoned with," he said.

The Steelers also managed a fairly big signing, wooing dual premiership winner Rod Reddy from St George. They also signed young halfback Greg Mackey from South Sydney. On the downside, new coach Smith rubbed foundation player Russell Holdsworth the wrong way and he decided to quit just before the season kicked off. "I cannot, and will not, play under Smith," he said. "I don't like his attitude. It's better to find out now we are not going to hit it off rather than later in the season." Holdsworth was involved in an unspecified incident during a pre-season training camp, which led to him paying a $2000 fine and apologising to the club in exchange for his release to go and play with Shellharbour in the local league.

The Steelers had a tough start to the season. With Newtown ejected from the competition, it gave every team two byes. But the Steelers' first week off didn't come until Round 11, by which time they were already sitting in 12th spot on just three wins.

One of those was the see-sawing Round Six match against the Bears, won 18-14 by the Steelers via a Greg Mackey intercept on the Illawarra line where he ran 85 metres to score. Bears players objected, saying they slowed down when they heard a whistle (believed to have come from the crowd).

The Round 15 clash against Penrith proved controversial. After the 18-10 loss, Smith almost became the first coach to be fined under the league's new rules about criticising referees.

"The better side didn't get the points today," he said. "We were clearly better. We had much the better game territorially and it was only two occasions when things went against us that cost us a win ... I can't say anything about the ref but today was a great example of the need for an in-goal adjudicator."

One of the two "things" Smith was referring to was Dorahy clearly being knocked down while trying to defuse a bomb early in the game. The Panthers gathered the ball and scored a try. "One of the touch judges told me he was coming in to report what had happened to me," Dorahy said, "but the try had already been awarded."

The second was referee Giles O'Donnell's ruling that Mackey had bounced the ball when scoring late in the game – that would have taken the Steelers to a 16-14 lead. "The ball flew in the air after I touched down," Mackey insisted.

"It was a try, but the ref's the boss."

Still, with one round to go, the Steelers were in with a shot at making the top five for the first time. A win over Manly in the last week would land them in a three-way tie for fifth with Souths and Canberra, necessitating several midweek playoffs to see who took the last spot (this was in an era before points differential were used to separate teams on the same number of competition points).

That last-round match was at Brookvale – a ground at which the Steelers had never won. That record continued, Manly outscoring Illawarra 34-10. It put that controversial loss to Penrith in a new light; a win there and the Steelers would have been in the playoffs for that last finals spot. Still the eighth-place finish and a 12-12 record suggested better times might be just around the corner.

That faith would be misplaced. In 1985, things went pear-shaped on and off the field. The club's finances didn't look great after Penfolds' sponsorship deal ended and the winemaker chose not to renew it. In August, the NSWRL, worried about the team's viability, began pushing for a move to the Campbelltown area. Newtown had tried to move there a season or two earlier and failed, while Western Suburbs were struggling and so the league didn't want to see the facilities at Orana Park at Campbelltown lie idle.

Not surprisingly, there was a lot of pushback from the Illawarra. What *was* a surprise was the support from Lord Mayor Frank Arkell who had previously seemed like a man who didn't much care for the hometown team. Maybe it was because he realised so many voters did.

"There's no bloody way the Steelers are going to

Campbelltown," he said. "We're in the NSW premiership, we'll stay in the NSW premiership and there's no way we'll merge with Campbelltown. The people of Wollongong and the Illawarra won't allow that to happen."

A supporters dinner was arranged for August 23 at the Wollongong Town Hall to canvass support. League bosses Ken Arthurson and John Quayle were invited. More than 600 people attended the dinner and they heard Arthurson say it would be a "crying shame" if Illawarra wasn't in the competition for the 1986 season.

"If the big business of the Illawarra and the people get behind the Steelers I feel certain you'll be there next year and still be there 20 years from now," he said. Well, he was half right.

There were machinations going on behind the scenes. Before the dinner, Lord Mayor Arkell had hosted a meeting of big business in the Illawarra. Representatives from BHP, Brambles, the ANZ bank and Lysaghts were all there.

It was from that meeting where a saviour arose, BHP boss Jerry Ellis saying he was "more than happy to talk directly with the Steelers club" about financial assistance. A week later the two groups were sitting down for talks and, by mid-September, the Illawarra steelmaker had signed a three-year sponsorship deal worth $100,000 a season. It was a union the club had hoped for right from the start; it was part of the reason they chose the "Steelers" name in the first place.

When it came to the premiership, the Steelers went backwards at a rate of knots. They won just five games in a season that saw a 10-match losing streak and gave the club its first wooden spoon.

One of those losses was against Cronulla at the Sharks' home ground in Round Five. Oddly, when the Steelers arrived, they found the walls of the visitors' sheds painted pink. It was a ploy from Sharks coach Jack Gibson, looking for an edge to get his team its first win. Gibson took a trick from psychiatric wards in the US where the walls are painted in soothing colours to calm people down. It clearly worked; the Sharks were up 20-8 in the second half, the final score of 20-12 only coming via a late try from the Steelers.

The following week, the Steelers lost to Wests at Lidcombe, sending them down to 11th spot, and they would stay way down the bottom of the ladder for the rest of the season. In Round 17, with nine rounds to go, the Steelers sat on the bottom of the ladder and stayed there for the rest of the season.

That went some way to explaining coach Smith's anger at the refereeing of Barry Barnes after a Round 17 loss to the Tigers. The Steelers were caned 13-5 in the penalty count, prompting Smith to tell the media "tonight everyone got to see why the Illawarra Steelers are on the bottom of the premiership ... when the whistle blows in the first five to 10 minutes you can tell, you can tell." At that point Illawarra officials stepped in and reminded Smith of the NSWRL's newly-introduced $1000 fine for criticising the officials.

There was some good news that came Illawarra's way for the upcoming season. Late in 1985, Sharks international centre Steve Rogers signed with the club. After a stint with St George in 1983-84, he returned to the Sharks but his season ended in the first match after the Bulldogs' Mark Bugden broke his jaw in a tackle. Bugden got 12 weeks and, five years later, Rogers took him to court. In evidence, Rogers told the court that, after the broken jaw kissing his wife was "not as enjoyable as it used to be". He won the case and ended up with a settlement of more than $70,000.

But back to 1985. Rogers was undoubtedly a big signing for the club; to this day he is widely considered the Steelers' best signing of all time. A routine call by Millward to player manager Greg Willett to see who was available for the 1986 season brought the news that Rogers wasn't happy with his offer from Cronulla.

Rogers liked Illawarra's incentive-based contract and signed up. But he would never play a game for the Illawarra side. He headed over to England to play with Widnes in the NSWRL off-season and broke his leg in his first match. Rogers tried to come good, even training with the Steelers in the first months of 1986 and watching his new team from the stands. But the injury was too serious and Rogers had to reluctantly retire.

6

That was the start to another frustrating year, one in which the Steelers pondered what might have been. While they came away with their second straight wooden spoon, their defence was among the best in the competition. Only four other teams – including the top three – let in fewer points than the Steelers. It was their attack that let them down – equal worst in the comp.

A high point in the seven-win season was a 22-8 win over the Dragons in Round 6. It was such a big deal, there was champagne corks popping in the dressing rooms afterwards. Quite literally – in a *Mercury* photo Ian Russell could be seen sipping from a bottle of champers. Centre Ken Daly wasn't among them; the debutante was at Port Kembla Hospital getting X-rays after having his jaw broken in a tackle.

"That win's been coming for a long time," Smith said. "My blokes didn't stop today when they had their opponents in trouble. They got stronger and kept going."

Off the field it was a challenge as well. In the 1980s, the NSWRL had shown it was willing to axe those clubs underperforming in a financial sense. At the end of the 1983 season, the Newtown Jets were punted just two years after making the grand final. Western Suburbs were meant to go at that time as well but took the league to court to earn their reinstatement. They were dumped again at the end of the 1984 season and again went to court. This time it was court delays over appeals that saved the club. The league was running out of time to compile the following year's draw and decided to include Wests. The club stayed in the competition for the '85 season. In October of that year, the High Court ruling stated the NSWRL had the right to expel clubs. But that decision came too late; again the league had already completed the draw for the following season, and again the Magpies were included.

So in 1986, the Steelers needed to ensure they were a going concern. The club felt one way of doing that was to become music promoters again – clearly not realising how lucky they were in 1984 that nothing went pear-shaped. The headliners for the January '86 show were Midnight Oil, supported by Spy Vs Spy and Strange Tenants, as well as local acts Mistaken Identity and Happy Accident.

There was a booze ban at the '86 show and Millward warned "smugglers" not to try and sneak anything into Brandon Park. "It doesn't matter how many times we say it – people still think they'll get a dozen cans or a bottle of bourbon through the gates," he said before the show.

The move meant security would search people for booze, which resulted in complaints of "heavy-handed" behaviour. "Security guards at the entrance gates confiscated all food from fans despite the fact that the well-publicised 'don't take' list included only alcohol, soft drink, glass and plastic containers," the *Mercury* reported the day after the concert.

Kerry Smith, who had travelled from Jervis Bay for the show, started a petition about the conditions at the show. "I'm a veteran of at least 50 outdoor rock concerts and I can honestly say that was the worst I have ever been to," she said. Smith claimed a security guard tipped out the contents of her handbag. "I was then forced to grovel on the ground amongst the crowd to pick up my personal belongings," she claimed.

The furore saw Millward swear it would be the last Brandon Park show for the Steelers. It caused further problems for the club with the Wollongong Licencing Squad recommending never granting the Steelers another liquor licence for an outdoor show unless improvements were made.

Things had gotten so bad that, at one stage during the concert, police had to close down the alcohol sales for two hours. Another issue that caught police attention was the lack of differentiation between tickets for purchasing soft drink, food and alcohol, meaning under-age fans could buy tickets for food and then use them to get beer.

Millward was not impressed with the suggestion that youngsters were buying booze. "I am adamant that underage patrons were not served with alcohol," he insisted. "Our information is that a great many of the underage drinkers arrived at the concert already drunk."

Also in the middle of the season the long-simmering issue of the Steelers' home ground boiled over. When the Steelers lodged their bid for inclusion in the NSW competition, there was talk of building a home ground at Kembla Grange. That never came to pass, but by 1983, the council was focused on a land swap deal with the state government, owners of the showground site.

The council would build a complex on the Brandon Park site (now home of Innovation Campus) and then do a swap with the government – Brandon Park for the showground. Then stage two of the council's plan would kick in; sell off a portion of the showground land to a developer to build a big fancy hotel on the site.

The Steelers went along with the idea of a new stadium at Brandon Park, largely because council offered the club a head lease, which meant they'd have oversight of the venue. But that offer was taken away so council could get state government funds to build the Brandon Park complex. That didn't sit well with the Steelers, who needed that lease arrangement to conform to NSWRL rules about eligibility.

In June 1986, the club greatly angered council by revealing plans for a $4 million redevelopment of the showground. Council hit the roof; they figured they had a deal with the club to move to Brandon Park– and they could see the windfall of a developer buying that waterside showground land for a hotel fading away. They were building this grandstand out at Brandon Park as part of that planned swap. If the showground was to be upgraded, then what was the point of Brandon Park?

"It is not possible to keep Wollongong Showground where it is," Lord Mayor Frank Arkell said, "and as the state's second city we deserve a much better facility instead of something that has just been patched up."

Council also pulled out a study in defence of the Brandon Park move that showed beach erosion at the showground was so bad that the site could end up underwater. "In a confidential report, tabled at Monday night's council meeting, aldermen were told beach erosion ultimately would affect the football field and other eastern areas of the ground," the *Mercury* reported. Though the council didn't raise the obvious question, if the showground was in such peril, why did they want a hotel built on the same site?

The centrepiece of the plan for the upgraded Wollongong showground was the reconfiguration of the playing field from an oval to a rectangle. In effect it would see the entire site move some metres west, moving the eastern fencing further away from the beach.

At a Round 17 match against Parramatta at the showground, the club handed out thousands of pamphlets stating its case. "The destruction of Wollongong Showground is not necessary ... and must not be allowed to happen." In his Sydney newspaper column the Eels' Ray Price gave his support to efforts to fix up a stadium he clearly hated. "The joint's a dive ... you get on the playing surface to find it's as hard as concrete, and has its share of pot holes. And when you get back to the dressing room there are three showers and one toilet."

He didn't blame the club; he sheeted the responsibility home to the council. By August the Steelers won, with the government announcing an upgrade of the showground.

The 1987 pre-season gave Steelers fans the chance to dream. The side won a pre-season competition that also included Newcastle, Penrith and Wests. Then they went on to win their two trial matches and the Round One match against Souths at Redfern – it was the first time they'd won their opening match of the season. When you took percentages into account, the Steelers were in the unusual position of top of the ladder.

Reality soon kicked in the door, the Steelers winning only one of their next six matches. That one win was a surprise 20-16 come-from-behind triumph over the Dragons. The side went into the sheds trailing 16-2, the boos of their supporters ringing in their ears, before returning to the field a different side, putting on 18 unanswered points.

"I feel relieved and very proud," Steelers captain Perry Haddock said. "That's the gutsiest win I've ever been associated with. We did the things right in the second half that we were supposed to do in the first half."

A Round Eight loss to the Panthers at Wollongong saw the local media give the club a serve. *Mercury* league reporter Charlie Richardson called the 18-8 loss "shameful" and threw in the worn-out cliché that the Steelers were a club in crisis. "In the opinion of many disappointed Steelers fans the club is headed for big trouble and only immediate and firm action by the board can avert a repeat of the disasters of the last two years," Richardson wrote.

"The Illawarra Steelers BHP board must take immediate action to discover what ails the club. Three years of the wooden spoon would be a tragedy."

The players bounced back the following week with a 32-12 thumping of the Magpies – after being down 12-2 at the break. They backed that up with the high point of the season. For the first time, the Steelers managed to defeat Parramatta, posting a 16-8 scoreline. It was a strange day for Steelers hooker Michael Bolt. Just 400 metres from the ground his MG sports car was a write-off after someone committed a U-turn in front of him.

He walked to the ground to be there in time for the kick-off, leaving a trainer with his wrecked car to pass on his particulars to the police when they arrived. Before he could play, Bolt had to take a breathalyser behind the grandstand. "It was a wonder no-one was killed," Bolt said. "My sports car is certainly in a mess."

After the match Smith decided to return serve at Eels coach John Monie over some perceived slight from last season. "In the past when we've come within an ace of beating Parramatta Monie has always come up with an excuse for why they only just beat us," Smith said.

"It has been the last game before the semi-finals or after a midweek cup game. Instead of giving us some dignity for a close game and solid effort, he said his players had their minds on something else or had key players on the sideline.

"Those statements are very trite and Monie is probably learning something right now. I would say that today he learnt that you can't always be a winner and that there's pride in playing well and losing."

It was a strange thing to say, especially given Smith was responding to something Monie said a year ago. But the 1987 season was one in which the Steelers coach showed he was very sensitive to criticism. In particular, he railed against the coverage the team got in the local media – seemingly forgetting that his team had come last two years in a row.

In the lead-up to the Round Six win over the Dragons he

urged his players to avoid the Wollongong media. "Locally a lot of the stuff has been garbage," Smith told *Rugby League Week*, "pretty much rumour sort of things. I don't think players need to read or listen to people being critical of them all the time."

The coach really let lose in the sheds after the Steelers snapped a four-game losing streak with a 12-10 win over Norths in Round 18. *Mercury* reporter Charlie Richardson claimed the coach called him a "fucking turkey" with 30 players and officials in earshot. Richardson also said Smith called his work "shit" and belittled him in a press conference.

Club officials wiped their hands of the incident. "We certainly don't condone any sort of personal attack, whether it be player or coach," Millward told Richardson. "But I feel what happened was between Brian Smith and you."

Smith's behaviour suggested the pressure had gotten to him, so perhaps it was for the best that he decided not to return for the 1988 season. Though he said he informed Millward of his intentions in the week before the Norths game and that locker room confrontation.

"At times it has been tough," Smith said of his time with the Steelers. "I've had to be realistic enough to say we've lost games because we haven't played well enough or the side wasn't coached well enough. But no-one could accuse me of not doing my best and I can leave Illawarra knowing it is a better club than when I joined."

It was a curious for him to say given the club had picked up two wooden spoons in his four years, had a negative points differential in each of those years and was on the way to finishing 11th in 1987.

Soon after a 24-4 home win over the Sharks, bulldozers and earthmovers took over the showground. Sponsors' generosity was footing a $1.2 million makeover, which included creating that much sought after rectangular playing field. Also, a hill was created at the southern end, apprentice bricklayers from BHP built stands at the northern end and a new scoreboard and lights were erected.

For the 1988 season, the board settled on Terry Fearnley as the replacement for Smith. Fearnley, who had previously coached Parramatta, Wests and Cronulla, thought about it for a few weeks, eventually agreeing to come on board as long as the club also signed Ron Hilditch as coach of reserve grade.

"I look at Illawarra now and it seems to be a lot like Parramatta in the '70s," Fearnley said. "The supporters there are like Parramatta's. It's a steel town and a dyed-in-the-wool rugby league town. It has a special feel to it. They were last in 1986 yet their home crowds averaged about 8000. There's a desperation to succeed among those people."

That point Fearnley was making with the crowd figures wasn't completely true. Yes, the 1986 home crowd average was around 8000 (7535 to be precise) but the fans didn't always stick by the club through thick and thin. A year earlier, when the club won the first of two consecutive wooden spoons, the home crowd average was just 5634. For each home game, roughly 2000 fans found something else they'd rather do with their weekend afternoons. But give them a winning side an they'd surely pack the joint.

Fearnley didn't give the region a winning side. The Steelers of 1988 were worse than the previous year, winning six games compared to the eight won in Smith's last season. Illawarra finished two spots lower on the ladder than last year at 13th – the only teams worse were newcomers Newcastle and Gold Coast as well as – no surprises – the Magpies.

It was a season that started with a loss to Canberra followed by a draw with Gold Coast (the Steelers also lost to them later in the year). The first win of the season came against big brothers St George at Wollongong. They took the game 20-4 aided by a 16-6 penalty count and an absence of the mistake-riddled efforts of the first two rounds.

The side went up and down over the next few weeks, until a Round Eight match at Newcastle which some said was the beginning of the end for the Steelers' 1988 season. Fearnley decided the team would travel up a day before the match and check in at a hotel. That night, he organised a team dinner, only to become dismayed when several players left the table to join another group.

Fearnley ordered them back and they all returned, with the reported exception of winger Alan McIndoe – who would become the club's first Kangaroo rep in 1988. Fearnley was ropeable and immediately dumped him into reserve grade, only to be talked out of it by Millward.

The Steelers boss saw that moment as when it all started to go wrong between the coach and players. "He didn't always get the co-operation of all the players that he demands as a coach," Millward said. "He was a few years older and he'd been out of the game for a while.

"He had difficulties with a number of players who refused to make adjustments to their game. They had become so set in their ways that it didn't matter what the coach thought, they believed their way was the only way."

At the mid-point of the season, Fearnley had had enough and wanted to walk. But Millward wouldn't let him go in the middle of the season and he was forced to see out the remaining games. The poor relationship between coach and players can be clearly seen in the downward spiral started by a 41-11 Round 12 flogging at the hands of the Bears.

Looking at the scorelines, it's hard not to conclude the players just gave up. The following week the Broncos thumped the Steelers at Wollongong 32-10, then headed to Penrith for a 36-2 flogging, followed by a 32-16 rout at Brookvale. That's a cumulative score of 141-39 over a four-week period.

The Norths' loss was on May 15 and the club didn't win another game for three months – a last round victory over the Roosters. The run of 11 straight losses was the worst in club history, eclipsing the 10 consecutive losses from the end of the 1982 season to Round Seven in '83.

At least off the field, the club had a big win. For several years, the board was keen to acquire its own licensed premises to help ward off any move by the league to punt them. They'd looked at the Oxford Hotel down the road from the showground and the Cabbage Tree Hotel in Fairy Meadow. When Wollongong city restaurant Don Camillo's came on the market, the club asked the NSWRL for a loan, but they said no. While supportive of the Steelers having a leagues club to remain competitive, the big bosses felt they'd need something more than a small restaurant with 10 poker machines.

In mid-1988, they found the perfect place – right across

the road from the showground. A block of land on the corner of Harbour and Burelli streets was up for grabs and so the Steelers pounced. The land was being sold by the city council, and the club offered $359,000 to be paid over 10 years. The council seemed okay with the offer, until a rival construction firm swooped in at the last minute and offered $320,000 and settlement within six weeks. That turned council's head and it felt there was better value for ratepayers to put the land up for auction.

That change of direction shocked the Steelers, with board chairman Brian Kurtz saying the move would see the demise of the club – the only major team without a leagues club; instead surviving on sponsorship and ticket sales.

"We undertook this project at the invitation of top council officers and they were very supportive in assisting us formulate our proposal," Kurtz told the *Mercury*.

"Now it appears the finance committee had destroyed the whole venture and killed our club in the process. They're holding a gun at our club's head; they might as well pull the trigger. We're talking about the end of the Steelers club – about nine years of hard work – and the end of major football in this region."

The council was perhaps not prepared for the anger that flowed from its auction plan – the *Mercury* in particular let them have it over and over again. There was also opposition from within with independent councillor Pat Franks questioning why council's head was turned by a lower bid.

Cr Alex Darling however, said council had no alternative. "It's a shame we couldn't aid the Steelers in this way but council must ensure top money when selling assets," he said, apparently overlooking the fact that the Steelers' offer was the higher of the two.

The about-face annoyed the Wingate family, who in May had decided to sell their neighbouring block to the Steelers even though a developer had offered them a higher price. That developer had wanted the block to build a restaurant and had offered the family $3000 more than the Steelers' maximum bid as well as free meals for the rest of their lives.

"It was a good offer but we wanted the Steelers to have it," Lloyd Wingate said. "We were heartbroken when we read they might miss out on their plans because of the greed of a few people on the council.

After weeks of conflict, council backed down and decided they would take the Steelers' money, voting to overturn its finance committee's recommendation to auction the land. It was Cr Darling who put forward the motion to give the club a 12-month option to purchase the land. "It was a great breakthrough for us after what has been a period of friction between us and council," Millward said.

It didn't take long for the Steelers to start coming up with the money. They launched a Foundation Gold Members scheme, selling lifetime memberships for $1000 a pop. They'd expected to get 250 people taking up the offer – instead 631 memberships were bought. It meant they could build a leagues club that would bring in much-needed revenue and, hopefully, allow them to attract high-profile players.

7

Excavation work started on the Steelers Club in April of the 1989 season. And it seemed the dream of a licenced club bringing in strong players had already become reality. That season saw the club snare Englishmen Andy Gregory and Steve Hampson. Gregory was the more eye-catching of the two; the halfback was a regular in the Great Britain side and had won a handful of premierships. But the other guy, fullback Hampson, was no slouch either; he'd played and won a few premierships and only injury had stood in the way of him representing his country.

However Gregory almost never played a game for the Steelers. His wife Dawn didn't like the beachside Towradgi unit the club had supplied and so Gregory decided they were going to head home. In a rush, the club managed to find a vacant unit overlooking Belmore Basin which was more to Dawn's liking and so they stayed for the rest of the season.

The deal had been stitched up before the start of the season. All the Steelers players – now under the helm of new coach Ron Hilditch – had to do was ensure they were in a good position on the ladder when the two Englishmen arrived in May. That absolutely didn't happen; by the time the new signings touched down at Mascot, the Steelers had lost their first eight games and were in last place.

"It will be a battle to get off the bottom of the table," Gregory said to the media at Sydney Airport. "There won't be any lack of effort from me and Steve. Hopefully we can make a difference."

It was to be the start of a dismal season where the club won just two games and ended up with their third wooden spoon.

It may have seemed the 1989 season was destined to end that way. After all, it started with boardroom ruction forcing Steelers chair Kurtz into resigning. He claimed there was pressure from key sponsor BHP to oust him, but representatives of the steelmaker claimed they hadn't called for his head. Though, curiously, a BHP senior accountant and board member took Kurtz's place.

Yet amidst the board room dramas and the on-field woes in the weekend competition, 1989 also saw a highpoint for the Steelers via the midweek Panasonic Cup. After years of subpar efforts, and amidst a season where they lost almost every weekend, on four Wednesday nights at Parramatta they gave Steelers fans a sense of pride in their team. Sure, they still lost in the end, but they went down swinging.

The 1989 midweek cup – four-quarter football played under lights – was the last year it was held, but it had been around under different sponsors' names since 1974. The competition included the Sydney teams but would also see other sides invited; country rep squads, teams from the Brisbane Rugby League competition or New Zealand. In the pre-Origin era, the mid-week comp was the only time Sydney league fans got to see the likes of Allan Langer, Wally Lewis and Mal Meninga. Those were players who were household names north of the border but little known to those who followed the Sydney comp.

The 1989 tournament saw appearances from a Port Moresby side, NSW Country and Combined Brisbane (even though the Broncos were also involved) – none of whom made it past the preliminary rounds.

As far as the Steelers were concerned, their first appearance under lights was March 29 when they met the Western Suburbs Magpies. The Steelers beat Wests 12-0, a win that was helped by the Magpies' performance, dubbed "dreadful" by coach John Bailey. The Steelers scored off two Wests' mistakes; a knock-on from the kick-off and penalty kick for touch that failed to find the line.

A day before the Steelers' May 10 quarter-final against Cronulla, Gregory and Hampson arrived. The imports rode the bench 24 hours after their arrival, only getting on the field at the back end of the match. By that time, the team had already dispatched the Sharks. Playing at Parramatta Stadium, Rodwell – who was playing his first full game of first-grade – scored a hat-trick of tries in a 40-0 drubbing of Cronulla Sutherland. "It's all new to me," the debutante said in the sheds after the game. "I've still got a lot to learn."

What made the 40-nil scoreline more impressive was that the points were scored in just three quarters of football – the first quarter was scoreless.

The win moved them into the semi-finals and a May 24 clash with North Sydney at Parramatta Stadium. By coincidence, the two teams had played in the Winfield Cup just days earlier; the Bears won 12-2. "The 12-2 loss in the mud last Saturday can be reversed," said Steelers captain Chris Walsh. "We're in the right frame of mind, we're all fit and we know we can do it."

But they almost didn't. In a tight contest, Norths took a 12-8 lead in the final quarter via a 70-metre try. It was as soccer-style kick from one of the Englishmen that helped the Steelers. In the fourth quarter, Gregory put a short kick through the Bears defence, chased it down and toed it forward again. Dean Schifilliti – who had called for Gregory to kick – got in on the act and kicked it again and then gathered the ball in to score. "I think I only touched the ball once with my foot," he said. "The ball then sat up and I had only one thought in mind. And that was 'don't drop the ball'."

The try levelled the score at 12-all, with the kick from Rod Wishart to take the Steelers two points clear. But the winger missed the conversion and the final score remained 12-12. That caused some confusion on the field; do they play extra time? Do they come back and play the game again? What happens? It turned out that according to the rules of the Panasonic Cup, in the event of a draw the winner was decided on a penalty countback. The Steelers, being on the right side of an 8-4 penalty count, were ushered through into the cup final on June 7.

It was the deepest an Illawarra side had gone in the midweek competition. The previous best effort was in 1978 from an Illawarra rep team picked from the local league competition. They beat Northern Division and Balmain to reach the quarterfinals, where they lost 12-2 to Easts.

The Steelers' opponent for the 1989 final would be discovered the following week in the other semi between the Brisbane Broncos and South Sydney Rabbitohs. The Rabbitohs were really up against it when they had to play the bulk of the last two quarters a man down. In the 47th minute winger Steve Mavin was sent off after kneeing Bronco Joe Kilroy, who had to be stretchered off the field.

At that point the Rabbitohs were already down 16-0 and losing Mavin made it too difficult to close the gap. The Broncos would easily make the cup final on the back of a 24-4 win.

There was a lot of money on offer in that midweek June 7 final. The cup winner would pocket $175,000 while the loser didn't go home empty-handed; they got a $110,000 cheque. There was the offer of some bonus cash for the Steelers as well. Just a day after the Broncos dispatched the Bunnies, Brisbane made a very, very cheeky offer. If the Steelers agreed to play the final at Lang Park, they would get half of the gate takings – estimated to be around $150,000.

Despite the prospect of some much-needed cash, the club said no. "There's no way we could possibly disadvantage or insult our rapidly increasing band of supporters," Millward said. In reality, the move could never happen – there was a rule in the mid-week comp that no team was allowed a home game.

Around the same time Bronco GM Jon Ribot noted the Steelers Round 7 clash at Lang Park – where the Steelers came back from 22-8 down to trail 26-24 – was one of Brisbane's toughest of the season. "In the match at Lang

Park, we had the Steelers on their heels and held a big lead," he said. "Next thing we knew, they had us rocking and neatly levelled the scores."

They'd end up being very prophetic words.

The city of Wollongong was fizzing with anticipation about the Steelers' first ever final. Scarlet and white was everywhere and the fans were happy for a silver lining around the dark cloud that had been the team's 1989 regular season.

Almost every bus in Wollongong had been booked to take fans up to Parramatta Stadium for the match. "Reports from bus companies indicate the support for the Steelers is unbelievable," Millward said. "I believe we'll have more than 5000 fans at Parramatta chanting for the Steelers."

State Rail also put on a Steelers Special train that would take people to Parramatta station and then they'd be bused to the ground. Tickets were $8 each and bookings were essential. The *Mercury* was deluged with entries in its competition to win one of 45 double passes to Parramatta Stadium as well as a return coach fare. Anyone not travelling up to the game could head to the town hall and watch it on TVs, "courtesy of Radio Rentals". Win or lose, the fans could hang around until 11pm when the players were expected to arrive.

But there was a potential problem looming. English half Gregory had missed the Steelers' Winfield Cup match just days earlier – a 18-6 loss to eventual grand finalists Balmain – with a broken bone in his wrist. That injury, which he picked up in the Cup game against Norths, could see him ruled out of the Cup final.

"Gregory's fitness is one of my major problems but I'm

hopeful we'll have him on the field on Wednesday night," coach Ron Hilditch said. "I'll check on his progress again tomorrow and maybe there'll be marked improvement."

Maybe the coach was trying to play a few mind games with the Broncos, but Gregory ended up being declared fit to play just 24 hours before the game. He wouldn't be the only one playing hurt; Rodwell and forward Les Morrissey had rib injuries while second-rower Dean Hanson had a knee ligament problem.

On the morning of the game, the *Mercury* ran a story claiming Brisbane coach Wayne Bennett said the Broncos would "stomp" all over the Steelers. It was gilding the lily quite a bit. Bennett was not the sort of coach to give an opposing side that sort of ammunition; what he said was that most of the Broncos players had big-match experience, having played State of Origin. The Steelers squad, not so much, and he wondered how the Illawarra players would cope.

"I've got the blokes to do the job," Hilditch replied. "They're not kidding themselves. They know the huge task ahead of them, they know what it will take to beat Brisbane. They'll do Illawarra proud."

It didn't look like that at the end of the first quarter of the Panasonic Cup final. The crowd at Parramatta Stadium was filled with scarlet and white, and the call of "Steelers! Steelers!" floated in the air. They booed Wally Lewis when he led the Broncos out of the tunnel, and cheered the Steelers.

About two minutes after kick-off, the crowd went quiet

when Joe Kilroy crossed in the corner for the Broncos after the Steelers gave away a few penalties to help their rivals march downfield. Then it happened again less than 10 minutes later with Peter Jackson crossing the line. Terry Matterson, who had missed the first conversion from out wide, slotted this one and the Broncos took a 10-0 lead.

Steelers captain Walsh got over the line late in the first quarter but was held up. It certainly wasn't the start the Steelers wanted and the crowd feared the floodgates had started to open.

The second quarter threatened to offer more of the same. There were holes right through the Steelers defence and it didn't take long for Brisbane to take advantage of those and send prop Sam Backo over to score. With the kick sailing through the uprights the scoreboard attention put up 16-0 Brisbane – and it surely was all over for the Steelers.

At that moment, the fans started worrying that maybe they shouldn't have come. They'd turned up to Parramatta Stadium in droves; scores of chartered buses and coaches had left Wollongong that afternoon, heading to Parramatta Stadium. Others took advantage of that train put on by State Rail. It would have been a late night for the kids on that ride; the train wasn't due to make it back to Wollongong station until midnight.

And it looked like that was going to be a very long, sombre trip back to Wollongong. With the second quarter of the 1989 Panasonic Cup final just a few minutes old the Brisbane Broncos were up 16-0. The crowd was silent, their thoughts gradually grew darker as the fear the Steelers were about to get flogged in their first big game after spending so long

Alive in the Five

trying to become a part of the Sydney league competition.

But then they got a bit of luck. Gregory drilled a grubber into the in-goal, which Kilroy fumbled. His hands pushed it up in the air, right as Rodwell ran past. The ball landed perfectly in his arms and he put it down for the Steelers' first try. Wishart landed the kick from out wide, narrowing the margin to 16-6. And suddenly, the crowd erupted, bellowing the "Steelers! Steelers!" chant.

Soon after, the Steelers got even more luck. With Brisbane on the attack inside the Illawarra quarter, Steelers centre Jeff Hardy was so far offside he was standing in the Broncos backline. That enabled him to take an intercept – and somehow not get called back by the ref or the touch judge. He sprinted past the halfway line and then offloaded to Wishart to take it the rest of the way. He was able to brush off chasing Bronco winger Michael Hancock and touch down under the posts. After he converted his own try, the score narrowed to 16-12. With Illawarra scoring two tries in six minutes, the worries Broncos boss Ribot had of a repeat of the Steelers-Broncos Round 7 comeback were coming true.

The half-time siren sounded at the worst possible time for Illawarra, with the Steelers on the attack again and looking likely to tie it up before going into the sheds. That siren helped the Broncos, who were looking a bit frazzled at the sudden onslaught of the Steelers.

Any efforts from the Broncos to regroup before the third quarter seemed to have come to nought as the Steelers kept the foot on the pedal in the third quarter. The scarlet and white made easy ground in the mid-field, taking full advantage of the one marker rule unique to the Panasonic Cup.

The Steelers came close to snatching the lead via a Gregory grubber into the in-goal but Ian Russell knocked on when trying to ground it. In the end, the only points in the third quarter came via a Wishart penalty goal after Gregory copped an elbow in the jaw from Hancock after a kick.

While the fans' tails were up going into the final quarter, a handling error from Russell sat them back in their seats and hushed them up. The Broncos picked up the loose ball and that led to Peter Jackson finding some space. He threw a volleyball pass over the heads of Steelers defenders and into the arms of Gene Miles, who crashed over for the try. With barely six minutes left on the clock, Matterson converted to take the visitors out to a seemingly insurmountable 22-14 lead.

Then long-time Steeler Michael Bolt made a valuable cameo. The first player to ever run onto the field as a Steelers player (he was third grade captain back in the club's debut season), Bolt came on as a replacement while Matterson was lining up the conversion for the Miles try.

Just minutes later, the Steelers had a scrum in the Broncos quarter, which Bolt managed to win against the feed. The ball found fullback Hampson, who threw dummies left and right before crossing over. Wishart slotted the conversion to bring it to a 22-20 margin, with just two minutes to go.

It was the second time in the match the Steelers had come back when most thought them done. So the fans hoped for a little something else, a little miracle. But there wouldn't be any such miracle for the Wollongong side; desperately throwing the ball around looking for a gap, looking for some space, they dropped the ball. The Broncos breathed a sigh of relief and then closed out the game they no doubt expected to be much easier than it really was. It was a game that certainly took it out of both teams, who would each lose their next regular season game. It may have taken a *lot* out of the Broncos, who managed to win only one of their next seven games.

"You should be proud of the way your blokes played," Broncos captain Wally Lewis told Steelers' Chris Walsh after the game. "They don't know the meaning of the word 'quit'. Other clubs would have turned it up when we got in front 16-0 but not your Steelers."

Despite the loss, the region was still proud of the Steelers effort. "You'll do us!" read the front page of the next day's *Mercury* over a photo of a smiling Chris Walsh ruffling the hair of Gregory. "Beaten, but not disgraced in Cup final," read the caption underneath the photo. It was a fair assessment too; the team that would win just two regular season matches all year had really gone much, much further in the Cup competition than even their most ardent fans dared dream.

"We gave them 16 points start," Gregory said, "and I'm as proud as anyone with our fightback. I'd sooner swap my Man of the Match award for a win tonight."

There was double the disappointment for Hampson and Bolt; they both returned to the sheds after the game to find someone had stolen their Steelers shirt and tracksuit. 'That's really weak," Hampson said. "I hope whoever nicked them is happy."

Both Hampson and Gregory would return home at the end of the season, the halfback not making good on his post-Panasonic Cup comment of "I certainly want to come back and play here again next year." Instead, he ended up with Widnes for the 1980 season. He stayed in the UK competition for the next 15 seasons.

But the club didn't need to look overseas to find the stars of the future, some of them had debuted that year. The 1989 season was the first for goal-kicking winger Rod Wishart, hooker Dean Schifilliti, forward Neil Piccinelli and the teenager Brett Rodwell (who the club named as Rookie of the Year, over Wishart). All would go on to become Steelers legends and be instrumental in what would be the club's greatest season just a few years later.

8

The biggest news of the 1990 season was the official opening of the Steelers Club on April 6. The venue was unusual in the NSWRL as it was the only club started by a top-flight team. Other teams had links to leagues clubs, but both remained quite separate entities.

NSWRL chair Ken Arthurson was impressed with the Steelers efforts of sticking it out for so long without the backing of a leagues club.

"From a personal point of view which is also that of a lot of other people in the game," Arthurson said, "I say that what the Steelers have been able to accomplish without a licenced club is absolutely unbelievable.

"They have been a high-profile club for many years without that support and I think that once the licenced club is running and going well, we are going to see a very strong Illawarra club."

Unlike the other clubs with a licenced premises, Millward wasn't expecting it to help fund the Steelers for the first few years, as it had a lot of loans to service. He knew the club would still need to largely survive on revenue from sponsorships and gate takings.

"Sponsorship will still be our backbone," he said. "We don't kid ourselves on surviving on crowds coming in for big home matches. That's only a few days out of the year so we'll have to be geared for the whole year round."

That inability to rely on people coming through the gates was proven in the first home game since the club opened – Round Four against Canterbury. Expecting a crowd of over 20,000, the rain put a dampener on the final figure with half that number turning up.

The game itself wasn't a great one for the Steelers either – the Bulldogs were comfortable winners 24-6. It gave the Steelers – still under the coaching of Ron Hilditch – a 2-2 start to the season. A first-round 11-10 win over Easts and a Round Three 41-6 flogging of the Gold Coast meant they had already equalled their total number of wins from the previous season.

It was a team made up of the youngsters that had proven themselves during the previous year's Panasonic Cup campaign. With the bulk of the club's money going to keeping them in the scarlet and white, there wasn't much left for outside recruitment in the off-season. The club picked up halfback Doug Delaney from Balmain, Wests prop Craig Teitzel, Souths' Darren Neville and Panthers utility Darren Currie.

In Round Six, the fourth-placed Steelers travelled to the Shire to face competition leaders, the Sharks. In a sign the young team had something to offer, the Steelers trounced Cronulla 26-14 after going into the break 16-2. And they did it without any help from the ref; they got their first penalty in the 79th minute.

After the game Hilditch spoke of the potential he saw in his side. "They are capable of making the semis," he said. "But I'm not going to declare us making the semi-finals."

The Sharks' return match at Wollongong in Round 21 was even more emphatic – the Steelers won 34-0. Providing motivation was the fact it was foundation player Michael Bolt's last match at home. At the end of the 1990 season, he'd played 212 grade games, 153 in the top-flight competition. At that time he also set the record for most consecutive first grade games at 187 (for the stats tragics, Bears half Jason Taylor (1992-2000) bettered that mark with 194, with Sharks and Titans forward Luke Douglas (2006-2014) setting a new mark with 215).

Bolt got to that 187 figure via a bench start in the Round 21 match against Cronulla after playing a game in reserves. In that reserve grade match he came good on a mid-week promise to kick his first goal in a league match. He missed an earlier sideline conversion but took a penalty shot five metres from the touchline and slotted it between the posts. Not content to stop at one goal, he managed to get first grade captain Chris Walsh to let him take a conversion from right in front – luckily for him it went over the crossbar.

The Steelers finished the season with a 10-6 win over St George at Kogarah. It was a gutsy win marred by the controversial send-off of captain Chris Walsh. Referee Neil Almond gave him his marching orders midway through the second half for striking Trevor Bailey with his foot while the Saints hooker held on in a tackle. In the sheds Walsh was upset about the decision – the first time he had ever been sent off since he started playing league at age seven.

"He had hold of my leg and I was just trying to play the ball," Walsh said. "If my foot did come down on him it wasn't meant because I don't play like that. It's just not my style of play. I was just trying to play the ball. Simple as that."

Admitting his was "an Academy Award performance" Bailey offered to go to the judiciary as part of Walsh's defence.

That last game of the season ended with a bang – literally. According to media reports Steelers lock Ian Russell set off a firework in the sheds after the match.

The 1991 season gave the club hope for the future. With 11 wins for ninth place, it equalled the highest final placing, achieved in 1984 (though not the total wins, the 1984 side won 12 matches). But the team was on the rise and the players coming through were growing in confidence. Among those was one of the best Steelers ever in the firework-lighting Russell. He hadn't had the best of starts with the Steelers, signing from Mittagong in 1986. He was late for training and became a player you couldn't rely on. So he spent most of his time in Third Grade and his contract wasn't renewed at the end of the year.

But the club kept an eye on him, deciding to give him another chance in 1988 – as long as he moved closer to Wollongong for training. He came back with a new sense of maturity and his running game and handy ability to offload the ball earned him a regular first grade spot.

In the 1990 season he won the BHP Medal, finished three points shy of the Rothmans Medal and was picked for the Kangaroos train-on squad.

Joining him in that squad were Walsh, Rodwell and Wishart (who also made his State of Origin debut in 1990). Add to that the season saw the debuts of John Simon and David Riolo and the future was looking good for the Steelers.

9

That future would be without Hilditch, who had decided to step aside after two seasons as coach. The man who had taken the team from wooden spooners to five points out of the top five in just two years would be hard to replace.

Former Test half Mark Murray was approached for the gig, though he would overlook the Steelers for the job of Easts coach. Steve Rogers was also mentioned as a possible starter. Ultimately, the club went with Hilditch's assistant Graham Murray. It was a good decision; he had built up a strong relationship with the players through the 1990 season. And he had a surprising connection to the Steelers in his background. Murray had worn the No7 for Souths in what was the Steelers' first ever win way back in 1982.

The Steelers put in a good show during the 1991 pre-season. They impressed people with their attacking play in the Sevens comp, reaching the semi-finals. They beat the Gold Coast and St George to make the Tooheys Challenge semi-final, where they lost to Brisbane.

That form deserted the team for their Round One home match against Penrith. Twenty minutes in and the game was already over; the Panthers led 22-4. When the full-time hooter sounded, the Steelers had lost 32-10 and found themselves in second-last spot on the ladder.

The scarlet-and-white managed to turn things around during their second-round match against Souths, winning 28-10, after leading 8-2 at half-time. Russell starred in the match; having returned to the run-on side after starting Round One on the bench. He didn't start the season on the bench due to reasons of injury; Russell had gone over to England during the off-season to play for the Sheffield Eagles.

"He came back from England late and had to earn his spot," Murray said after the Souths win. "He's done that; he'll be the first bloke picked for the Canterbury game [the following week]."

The match was also memorable because it marked the late debut of Paul McGregor. Late, because he was 23 when he ran out against Souths. Enjoying playing for the Dapto Canaries with his mates on Saturday afternoon had been just fine for him. McGregor wasn't particularly interested in giving that up and so had politely rejected the Steelers' regular overtures.

While he did play one reserve grade match for the Steelers in 1989, his lack of interest was shown by the fact he left with the crowd after the game. Still, the Steelers waved an $8000 offer to become a Steeler at the end of the 1989 season, but McGregor again said no.

Things changed a year later, when Dapto won the local league premiership. After climbing that mountain, McGregor went back to Millward and said he was ready to have a crack at first grade. In a risky – and possibly foolhardy – move,

Millward told him the offer was now $5000. The centre dubbed 'Mary' since he was 12 (though the Steelers would soon launch a failed campaign to change it to something more masculine, like Buster) wasn't impressed, but still took the offer.

Round Three saw the Steelers deliver a hiding to the Bulldogs at Wollongong, 44-2. Wishart equalled the single-match pointscoring record with a try and eight goals while half John Simon easily controlled the game.

The two-game win streak ended with a dour 2-all draw against the Sharks. Both teams had a chance to win the game from the boot alone; Wishart kicked one from two while the Sharks' Alan Wilson had four penalty shots but could only land one of them. After the game, Queensland-born hooker Dean Schifilliti bemoaned being left out of the Origin train-on squad, saying that being with the Steelers meant he was out of sight, out of mind. "I don't think I'm any chance in rep football," he said. "But I'm just happy to keep playing well. The blokes here appreciate me."

The next two matches were wins to the Steelers, and saw that at least Sydney selectors had been paying attention to what was happening in Wollongong. Russell, Wishart and Rodwell were picked for the Country Origin side, while Simon made City Firsts (McGregor later joined him after playing just five matches when Chris Johns failed a medical).

Maybe it was the highs of rep selection but the Steelers crashed to earth in a lacklustre 16-2 effort against Newcastle. Rather than tear shreds off his team, Murray didn't even make them watch a tape of the game.

"I reckon this mob here – and I've only been in the joint

for two years – get punished in the press very severely when they do something wrong. I made a promise to myself not to be negative with these blokes and rather dwell on the positive. That was the reason I didn't show them the video. There were a lot of negative things to come out of that."

Murray's tactic worked; the Steelers ripped through the Seagulls the following week posting their second 40-plus scoreline. They flogged the hapless Gold Coast 46-4, with McIndoe (who had returned to the Steelers via the draft after two years in Penrith) breaking the club record for most tries in a match with five. It also served to throw some egg on the faces of Queensland Origin selectors, who had chosen to leave him out of their calculations.

The 1991 season was also one that included a few controversial moments, which prompted some to believe the Steelers were robbed of a premiership place. The first of those controversies came in a Round Nine match against Wests at Campbelltown. The Illawarra side lost 13-12, via a late field goal from Magpie fullback Shaun Devine. The Steelers claimed Devine was shepherded by team-mates while lining up the one-pointer, and also complained about a forward pass leading to Wests' second try. All of which overlooked the fact the Steelers let Wests get out to a 12-0 half-time lead.

"There were a number of penalties [in the first half] I wasn't happy with because we gave them away," Murray said. "You just can't stand in front of the referee and expect him not to penalise you."

On the upside of the ledger, Neil Piccinelli set a new tackling record, hitting the Magpies 57 times in the match.

"When Piccinelli tackles it's not a flop," Murray said. "It's not a third man in. He tackles them one-on-one. If he's done 57 then that's what it is."

The other match that raised the hackles of Steelers fans and officials was the Round 16 fixture against Penrith. Going into the game, the Steelers were in the top five, where they'd been since Round Five (barring a week in Round 15 where a lost to the Eels saw them drop to sixth) taking on the No1 team.

With six minutes left on the clock, Wishart slotted a penalty goal to put the Steelers in front 20-18, after the Panthers led 12-2 at the break. Soon after, Rodwell got up to play the ball close to his own line. Marker Mark Geyer gave Rodwell a shove, which jarred the ball free. But referee Bill Harrigan had been looking away at the crucial moment, turning his head back to see the ball on the ground. Geyer had picked up the ball and offloaded to winger Darren Willis, who scored in the corner. In an era before touch judges were miked up and took a more active role, the call was left to Harrigan, who ruled Rodwell had spilled the ball and the try was fair.

In the sheds, Rodwell said captain Schifilliti spoke to Harrigan about the incident on the field. "I did get pushed but you get a bit of a push and a shove in every play the ball," Rodwell said. "It was just one of those things. I don't think the referee saw it because he was behind the markers and didn't actually see the situation."

The club vowed to place the incident in its official match report, while later that week Harrigan admitted he'd made a mistake. In hindsight, fans pointed to this moment as costing the Steelers a finals berth, because the team finished two points out of the top five but the reality is a little more complex than that. After the Willis try, the Steelers let Penrith cross the line again, clearly showing that the controversial try wasn't the difference between a win and a loss.

Also, 1991 was an era before the league decided to use points differential to split teams who finished with the same number of point on the ladder. Instead, the tied teams had to play against each other in a mid-week match to see who went through to the finals.

In 1991, Wests and Canterbury both finished on 27 points, and had to play on the Tuesday night to decide who took fifth spot (it was Wests). The Steelers finished two points behind both of them. Had the Steelers not been "robbed" of those two points against Penrith, it wouldn't have seen them automatically in the finals; they would have finished equal with Wests and the Dogs, meaning they had to play one, maybe two, midweek matches – and win them – to make it into fifth spot. The Steelers lost their only game to Wests that year and split their two match-ups with the Dogs, so a final berth was far from a certainty.

Still, a best ever 12-win, one-draw season and eighth place finish hinted at better things to come. As did the club's ability to lock in key players for the coming season. Wishart (who had become the Steelers' first test player in 1991), as well as being named Dally M winger of the year, re-signed with the club during the year, as did Rodwell, McGregor, Russell, Piccinelli and Schifilliti.

The coming 1992 season was sure to see the Steelers just

continue to get better.

10

In preparation for the 1992 season, the Steelers let it be known they were looking for some big-name talent in the engine room. Names like Mark Geyer, Brent Todd and Glenn Lazarus were on the shopping list – though the club could only afford one of them. "We've made it quite clear that, if we can get a couple of top-class forwards to add to the forwards we've already got we will improve our side," Millward said.

History will show they didn't get any of those players. Instead they picked up forwards Steve Waddell from Penrith, Craig Izzard (formerly of Panthers, Eels and Tigers) and Dave Gallagher from Wests. None of them were ever going to be mistaken for a "top-class forward". But they did the job. And, in 1992, history would also suggest the Steelers didn't exactly need a top-class forward.

Leading into the 1992 season, Murray took issue with the line of thinking that was common around the team – and the city. Months after the end of the 1991 season, many still held that belief the Steelers were robbed off a finals sport due to the controversial loss to Penrith – and also against Wests.

"It's been said over the off-season that if we had beaten Penrith and if we had beaten Western Suburbs we would have made the semi-finals," he said.

"I think just now we have to stand up and be a little more accountable for ourselves and our actions on the football field. Sure that wasn't too kind for us at Penrith and I'm the first to admit that on behalf of the players and myself. But I'm not going to stand here and say 'if we beat Penrith that day …' because I think we had enough chances to beat sides like Parramatta and Canterbury and we let them get away."

The message was clear – take responsibility for your losses and stop looking for someone else to blame.

Really, no-one remembers who wins pre-season competitions. In fact, most people don't even remember the pre-season competitions themselves. Well, no-one except the fans of those teams without anything to speak of in the trophy cabinet. For them, taking out a competition where other sides are approaching it as little more than a glorified trial counts. It totally counts.

For the Steelers, the 1992 Tooheys Challenge totally counted. It didn't matter that the games were played in rugby league outposts like Wagga Wagga, Bathurst, Dubbo and … umm … Nambucca Heads. It didn't matter that some teams clearly weren't trying too hard (the Roosters lost 30-6 to the Gold Coast, who would not score that many points in any of it 1992 regular season matches while on their way to their second straight wooden spoon). Nothing matters when you come home with a trophy that showed you won something.

Alive in the Five

The knockout-style competition started in late February with all 16 teams taking part. In Round One Illawarra travelled to Lismore to take on Parramatta as the first half of a double-header (the second game being Souths and Canterbury). The Steelers took down the Eels 10-8. But the win came with a heavy price – goalkicking winger Rod Wishart picked up a hamstring injury and would miss the remainder of the pre-season tournament. Fullback David Riolo hurt his knee and first choice hooker Dean Calloway was injured too.

All three – along with half Doug Delaney, who buggered his ankle at training during the week – would miss the match-up with Souths at Bathurst. Though on the bright side, McGregor would play his first game for the club after off-season shoulder surgery. The game was a seesawing affair with Souths up 8-4 after the first quarter, the Steelers ahead 16-14 at the long break before Souths reclaimed the lead 22-18 at three-quarter time. A try to rookie Ryan Girdler nine minutes from full-time gave the Steelers the win. But it was the work of winger Alan McIndoe that coach Graham Murray singled out. Not only did the winger score two tries but he made sure youngsters like Girdler and Brendan O'Meara didn't get overwhelmed. "That was terrific," Murray said. "The young blokes might be feeling the pace a bit too hard and start to feel a bit sorry for themselves. Then McIndoe sings out, 'Get up here'. It's good."

The win meant the players had to find their passports because they were off to Auckland to play the Sharks for a spot in the final. The Steelers took an early lead after Andrew Ettingshausen spilled the ball and John Simon swooped. He managed to tunnel through some underwhelming defence to go into the first break up 4-0. Cronulla evened the score early in the second half, but they also missed the conversion. In a somewhat dour defensive game, there wouldn't be another point scored until Brett Docherty crossed in the 66th minute to take the score to 8-4. The fill-in fullback then saved the game a second time when he grassed a runaway Ettingshausen with just minutes on the clock.

It put them into the final, which coach Murray felt was a great result given the high injury toll – there were five first grade backs who had been hurt during the pre-season series. He felt the teenagers who took their places had really stepped up.

"To be able to put good young blokes in who have hardly had any experience and they come up for you, that's the thing I'm pleased about," he said after the win over Cronulla. "I had no doubt they were going to be ready."

The win set up a final against Brisbane at Dubbo, the team who heartbreakingly beat them in the 1989 Panasonic Cup final. Even with the chance of the team's first trophy in sight, Murray wasn't getting ahead of himself.

"We haven't won too many things in our history and we've still got some bad memories of that 1989 loss," he said. "It's too early in the season to predict a final-five position but we've improved on last year and have more depth. I'm positive."

Steelers CEO Millward had an eye to the bottom line, noting the prizemoney on offer – $200,000 for the winner and $130,000 for the runner-up. The players probably were too; the Steelers' policy for non-Winfield Cup prize money was to split it 50-50 between the club and players. A win against Brisbane would mean each player in the 17-man squad would pocket close to $6000 each. "It will be a big payday for the players and also a big boost for the club," Millward said.

He also rated the team's effort in reaching the final as more impressive than the 1989 mid-week comp. "To make that final in 1989, we had one easy win against Cronulla and a reasonably easy game against Wests," he said. "We had to fight hard against Norths in the semi-final to get to the final. But in this one we've really had to fight hard in each game – Parramatta, Souths and now Cronulla."

It would be a short turnaround for the Steelers; the win over Cronulla was on a Tuesday night and the final was five days later on the Sunday. Brisbane planned to fly to Dubbo on the Saturday, but the Steelers would stay home and catch a plane on the morning of the game.

In his match preparation, Broncos coach Wayne Bennett said he wasn't interested in watching a tape of the Steelers-Sharks match. "I don't know how the Steelers went against Cronulla," the coach said. "I won't worry about them too much. They won, that tells me enough.

"I have enough trouble getting my own side's preparation right without worrying about what Illawarra is doing. If we play somewhere near our potential we'll be okay."

Murray's key concern was whether some players would make it through a fitness test on Sunday morning. Test wingers Wishart (hamstring) and McIndoe (bruised ribs and a sore ankle) needed to get over their injuries, as did half Mick Neil and second-rower Izzard. In the end, only Wishart would miss out, though he still came along for the plane ride to Dubbo.

The game was held in the late afternoon on Apex Oval, where the dressing sheds must have been quite some distance from the field. Both sides had to run around 50 metres between two rows of kids reaching out over a waist-high fence to touch the players. Chris Walsh led the Steelers out first, the team wearing their white away strip. Then they milled about on the field, waiting for the Broncos to make their way through the kids' sea of hands.

While the Steelers had no problems with the children' keenness to reach out and touch a big-time rugby league player, the Broncos weren't into it at all. Allan Langer led his side out, running with his torso turned at a 45-degree angle as if to avoid anyone touching him. Some of his team-mates followed his example, one of them angrily swinging his shoulder away from hands that were reaching out to him.

The scoreboard attendants ended up with a lot of free time in what became a low-scoring affair. Docherty kicked the Steelers two points ahead in the ninth minute after referee Bill Harrigan ruled the Broncos offside. He added another 11 minutes later when Langer was offside after regaining a John Simon chip kick that had hit a Broncos player. The sides went into the first break with the Steelers up 4-0.

Early in the second quarter, the Steelers gave away one of the dumbest penalties you're likely to see. McIndoe was at dummy half and decided to go for a run. Only problem was, Simon was coming back onside and, for some head-scratching reason, chose to walk right alongside the play the ball. And straight into McIndoe, who was forced to fend the half out of the way. Harrigan pinged McIndoe for a shepherd and kicker Terry Matterson piloted the ball between the sticks to close the margin to 4-2.

And from that point the scoreboard attendants could have gone off for a beer and a pie. In the remaining 58 minutes of the match, not another point was scored. But that didn't mean the game was dull. It was, at times, a frenetic game, with line breaks made by both sides only for either desperate defence or a mistake in attack seeing it come to nothing. Several times the Steelers kicked ahead rather than looking for the unmarked team-mate looming up next to them. While the team couldn't score a try, they weren't going to let the Broncos in either. Late in the game there was a much-needed tackle from teenager Girdler on Tony Currie, who had made a break down the sideline. But in terms of trysavers, nothing beat the skinny Riolo's tough hit on Willie Carne.

Eight minutes after Matterson scored the Broncos' only points, Langer put up a kick for winger Carne, who caught it five metres from the corner and seemed certain to score. The tiny fullback Riolo swooped in, laying a shoulder on Carne and putting him into touch right at the corner post. It was so close to a try that, in the modern era, the bunker would have needed several replays to decide whether the Broncos winner had scored. That trysaver was part of the reason the skinny fullback was named player of the match.

While there is no such thing as a single turning point that determines the outcome of a match, Riolo's tackle certainly kept the Steelers in the game. Plus, it showed that Illawarra were taking this pre-season game on a country footy oval very seriously indeed.

There was an extra reason for the Steelers players to be happy. When the full-time hooter sounded it meant the Steelers had held the Broncos tryless in their last two clashes (in Round 14, 1991, the Steelers won 19-2).

"Tonight, they've overcome their nemesis," Ray Warren said in commentary at the end of the match, "with a four points to two victory. Congratulations to them, they've won their first big title since joining the Winfield Cup brigade of teams."

Years later Murray would recall the importance of the win to the Steelers. "Even though the scoreline might suggest it, it certainly wasn't a dour affair," Murray said. "The Broncos were hailed as a tremendous attacking football team going into that season and I remember it was quite open football. It was late in the afternoon in Dubbo, it was quite humid and we were hanging on for dear life."

In an odd footnote, after the first round of 1992 Murray got a letter in the mail from a league fan complaining about the Broncos' jerseys which had the players' numbers placed on top of a square plastic patch. The fan's contended this was an unfair advantage as it made the players' jerseys harder to grab onto.

Murray got a copy of the letter – which also went to the NSWRL – by virtue of the Steelers having played them in the pre-season final. Never mind the obvious problem; that the plastic patches didn't help the Broncos win that game.

Broncos CEO John Ribot saw it for what it was – ridiculous. "It's got to be a joke. We've played 30 first grade games for the last four years and now someone says we've got an advantage because of the plastic on our jumpers? It has to be a hoax."

Hoax or not, the league didn't give the complaint much attention either.

11

When a team kicks off their season there are two things they don't want; to draw what was steadily becoming a bogey side, and to have top graders out injured. But that's what the Steelers faced in Round One, having to make the trip up the coast to play the Knights in Newcastle. Going into the 1992 season, they'd played each other five times, the Steelers losing more than they won.

Missing from the run-on side for the start of the season were the likes of Rodwell, Wishart, Piccinelli and new signing Neil. Of those, Piccinelli's injury was the worst – and the oddest. During the off-season he was on the waters off Era Beach in the Royal National Park hauling up lobster pots. The propellor of his boat got tangled up in a pot line as the forward was pulling it up. Holding onto the pot line as a wave passed, Piccinelli's thumb got caught. The digit was cut in two, with only the skin holding it together. It was an injury that saw him sidelined for the Tooheys Challenge triumph and would leave him waiting until Round Nine to make his debut.

With key players out for both the pre-season and the start

of 1992 competition, it gave youngsters and newcomers a chance to stake their claims. Among those was ex-Wests player Docherty and teenager Girdler. The latter had debuted off the bench during a home game against Souths the previous season, but the First Round clash against the Knights was his first time in the run-on side.

"I got a taste of it and now hopefully I can carry on in the Winfield Cup," Girdler said in days before Round One. "The pace of first grade is a lot faster than 21s or reserve grade and I think learning what the players do, how to follow them and expect what Russo [Ian Russell] and them do takes time to adjust to a side."

The performance of the replacements was good enough that Murray could move Dale Fritz (who had been sitting for exams in his job as a metallurgy student with BHP in the days before the Newcastle clash) from the centres to his preferred position of five-eighth. It also meant Test player Wishart was forced to make his return from a hamstring injury off the bench.

"Normally, he would be selected in any starting line-up in any of the 16 Winfield Cup teams," Steelers operations manager Neil Lovett told the *Mercury*. "But it would have been very difficult for Graham to leave out any of the players who performed as creditably as they did in the Tooheys Challenge final."

In an indication that something special was expected of the 1992 season, City Rail went to the trouble of creating a Steelers Special train to Newcastle on match day. Punters could pay for the train ride up and back – but they still had to buy their own tickets to the match itself.

Wishart would end up taking the field, replacing Docherty in the 32nd minute, leaving in the 67th minute. Just a few minutes after taking the field, he popped a pass for John Cross to score the Steelers' first try, and kicked two goals. With the Knights attacking close to the line, Fritz intercepted a pass meant for Paul Harragon, pinned his ears back and set sail for the tryline at the other end of the field. He was grassed metres short by winger Ashley Gordon, but from the play the ball, dummy half Wishart flicked it to Cross to score under the posts.

Late in the match it looked as though the Steelers were going to start their season 1992 ledger with a loss. The Knights were up 14-8 and looking to hold out the visitors until the final siren. But Russell had other ideas; he took on the line and then popped a short ball to put Schifilliti into a gap in the defensive line. The hooker dove over the line near the posts, and Docherty – who was back on the field for Wishart but had missed two earlier penalty attempts – slotted the conversion for a 14-all scoreline.

From there, a field goal seemed the obvious play, but the Steelers kept pushing for a try; kicking the ball behind the defence rather than set up for the one-pointer.

"I think the players thought they were going to score but there was a bit of a mix-up with the call," Murray said. "Johnny Simon thought he was going to get the ball to have a pot at it but they went left and thought they were going to score from another kick."

In the end, the siren sounded before either team managed to break the deadlock; in the era before golden point, it meant each side went away with one point. Rather than chip

Alive in the Five

his team for missing the chance for a field goal, Murray chose to see the glass as half-full. "It was always going to be tough up here. We expected a tough game and weren't disappointed. The scoreline tells it all. It was a result most teams will be happy to achieve in Newcastle.

"You've got to be realistic about it – Newcastle's going to beat plenty of sides on their home ground. So to get one point is okay."

The coach also praised the efforts of new signing Izzard, who he felt was the standout performer on the day and made a few fans eat their words. "It was pleasing to hear a couple of supporters who had been critical of the club for originally signing Izzard actually come forward and give him a wrap," Murray said.

The day after the match came the reason Wishart had to be replaced in the 67th minute – he had reinjured his troublesome hamstring. "Once Rod went on the plan was to use him for the full time," Murray said, saying the injury was a concern for the club. "We'll just have to go without him if he's not right. He certainly turned things around while he was out there, pulling off a couple of great tackles and they started to feel his presence. I wish we could have him for 80 minutes but it's not to be at the moment."

It wouldn't be until Round Five that Wishart would return the field, in a season where injuries and rep duty meant he would play just 12 games.

Yet another injury to a side that had already had more than its fair share came to light during the preparation for the

Steelers' home debut against the Sharks. Somewhere during the match against the Knights, McGregor had worn one around the chops, losing a tooth and also cracking a wisdom tooth. While early in the week there were thoughts he could play, by Thursday he was under the anaesthetic at Illawarra Private Hospital.

"It's disappointing to say the least," McGregor said out of a presumably still-swollen face. "I was just starting to get going again."

It called for yet another reshuffle. After starting as five-eighth a week earlier, Fritz found himself back in the centres, with Russell pulling on the No6 jersey. That, in turn pulled the up-and-coming Cross off the bench and into the starting line-up. Forwards Craig Teitzel and Dave Gallagher were added to the bench to provide some size come interchange time.

"We had a tough tussle with them in Auckland," Murray said, referring to the Tooheys Challenge match against the Sharks earlier in the year, "and I anticipate they'll come at us through the forwards, so I just wanted to pick some coverage in that area."

The Sunday afternoon match marked the official opening of the 4000-seat Merv Nixon stand, at the southern end of the showground. Wollongong was perhaps the only NSWRL team to have a grandstand named after a trade unionist; Nixon was immortalised by the Showground Trust for his work in the early 1980s to save the venue from demolition.

Aside from the grandstand's official opening, Girdler provided the only other bright spot in what the *Mercury*'s Mike Gandon described as a "drab day of mistake-riddled football". The centre who was fast catching the eye of other clubs, scored in the ninth and 24th minute. His second showed the teen's quickly developing sense of support play. Schifilliti split the markers found Cross who then found open space. Drawing the last line of defense, he cut out Les Morrissey and connected with Girdler who had been trailing the play in the hope of touching down.

With Docherty's two conversions, the Steelers went into the sheds at half-time 12-0 up. And didn't score a point in the second half. It obviously didn't help matters that yet another injury cropped up; Russell left the field about 20 minutes in and didn't return. Still neither side was happy with the way they played, though the Steelers could at least comfort themselves with the 12-4 scoreline.

"We didn't play all that well but I'll take the two points," said Steelers captain Walsh. "There were a lot of mistakes and the coach wasn't too happy with the way we played. It's important that even when you don't play that well you still get the two points."

It was two points that saw them climb into the top five for the first time this season; a place that would soon become their regular home.

The Steelers game at Tweed Heads against the Seagulls in Round Three was, to put it bluntly, a bit of a mess. It was full of send-offs, sinbins, suspension, a headbutt and, in the end, no-one got any competition points. Broadly speaking, the Gold Coast Seagulls were a bit of a joke; since joining the NSWRL in 1988, they had found a home for themselves at the bottom of the ladder. Their highest finish was equal third-last in 1989 (back when they were called The Giants) and 1992 marked the middle of a threepeat of wooden spoons.

However, at the start of the 1992 season, the Seagulls looked like they might have something. Something aside from Wally Lewis, that is; who in the last year of his professional career was serving as captain-coach (probably the last ever NSWRL player to do so). Lewis was still a contributor, but they had more than just him. In the 1992 season, the club had opened up the cheque book and signed premiership winner and Australian rep Dale Shearer, dual premiership winner and New Zealand rep Brent Todd, as well as Raiders' grand final hero Steve Jackson and St George utility Peter Gill.

They had some talent; and their results over the first two rounds hinted at that. While they hadn't won a game, they'd lost by just six points to Manly at Brookvale (28-22) and Brisbane at Lang Park (24-18). Both efforts were worthy results against top flight opponents.

None of which is meant to excuse the Steelers losing 18-8. The visitors should have accounted for the Seagulls; given the home side lost a player less than a minute in. After just four tackles, Todd collected David Walsh high and referee Eddie Ward said "nope, not having any of that. Off you go, sunshine". Now, with the Seagulls having to play a man short for almost the entire match you'd be pretty confident they'd lose right? Well, the Steelers certainly appeared to think that, playing like the game was already theirs because they had the extra man. Confounding expectations, it was the Seagulls who lifted; their scrambling defence shutting down the Steelers, their attack putting first points on the board via a try to fullback Danny Peacock.

The Steelers also should have been down a player when, late in the half, Les Morrissey unleashed a headbutt on Gill. It wasn't a glancing blow either, Morrissey wound up and really delivered. Yet somehow Ward didn't think it was worthy of a send-off, much to the understandable annoyance of the Seagulls.

In the second half, the Steelers started unravelling more; after an admittedly dodgy try to Seagulls' half Jason Twist, Schifilliti was binned for unleashing a spray at Ward. By that time, even though the Gold Coast were only 12-8 in front, the game was effectively over.

Perhaps the only bright spot for the Steelers was a sparkling long-range effort sparked by Riolo that almost led to a try. The Steelers fullback fielded a Shearer kick deep in his own half and then ran it back 50 metres straight through the middle of the Seagulls defence. On the Gold Coast quarter, he linked up with Girdler, who evaded a grab from Peacock and looked set to score. But as Peacock fell, he swiped a hand at Girdler's ankles, tripping him up short of the line.

With the Seagulls up 18-6 in the dying stages, they still weren't 100 per cent sure they would get the win. That was evidenced by the amount of players suddenly coming down with leg cramps when trying to play the ball (funny how players in defence never seem to get those game-slowing cramps). They needn't have bothered; there was no way the Steelers were going to leave Tweed Heads with the win.

In a strange twist to a strange game, the Seagulls ended up being docked their two competition points for an illegal replacement. The side had used five replacement players rather than the four allowed, the extra player covering for someone in the blood bin. It seems some teams were still having trouble working out all the little rules around the newly-introduced blood bin.

"It appears there is still quite a bit of confusion over the blood bin rule," said league boss John Quayle, "and this is the first time this matter has come up since it was introduced a year ago." Despite the feeling it was a simple mistake and that the league would go easy; the NSWRL took away the Seagulls' points.

In the wake of the Tweed Heads match, the Steelers would be without the services of Russell for a fortnight after he was suspended for two weeks for a high tackle on winger Clinton Mohr. "I came across in cover defence as a five-eighth and I didn't think he was going to pass inside," Russell told the judiciary. "He unloaded the ball and I was committed to a shoulder charge."

As well as putting in doubt his chances of being selected for the upcoming City-Country match, it also ruled Russell out of that year's Rothmans Medal, in which he had polled well over the previous two seasons.

12

Meeting the three-time grand finalists and Premiers in 1989 and 1990 sounds like it would be a difficult task. But the Canberra Raiders of 1992 were not the same Green Machine of recent seasons; the flouting of the salary cap had seen to that. In 1992, they had to offload a number of players; not all their stars, obviously, but enough first graders to affect their onfield results in 1992. The likes of Glenn Lazarus, Brent Todd, Nigel Gaffey, David Barnhill, Mark Bell and other went elsewhere.

The result was a team that would finish in 12th position in 1992, losing more games than they won. Coming into their Round Four clash with the Steelers at Wollongong, the Raiders had beaten the Premiers Penrith in Round One, but followed it up with losses to Manly and Brisbane. Against the Steelers, the Raiders would be without key players Laurie Daley, Ricky Stuart and Gary Belcher.

The Canberra match was a big deal for Andrew Pauls, who had been called up to make his first-grade debut in the centres after Fritz had been moved back to the No6 jersey to replace the suspended Russell. He would find himself lining up against a guy called Mal Meninga. "If I thought I ever would make first grade, I never thought I'd be up against the best centre in the world," Pauls said. "So it's come as a real big shock to me. I respect Mal but I will be going out there to do my best."

Pauls didn't end up on the scoreboard, but plenty of his team-mates did. The Steelers ran in five tries in a strong 29-10 win. Twenty-five of those point were laid on in a blistering first half. John Simon was singled out for praise, with the *Mercury* saying the teenager produced it all, "pinpoint kicking with both left and right feet in general play, slick passing, speed in a scintillating 60-metre try and shuddering defence on opposition forwards and backs". It was surely enough to earn him a spot in the upcoming City-Country match.

Also called up for the game was regular fill-in forward Gallagher in what was his first full game in the Winfield Cup. "I ran out of puff in the second half because that was my first full game since Parramatta about eight weeks ago," he said. "I struggled on and we got there."

Even though the Raiders were without most of their marquee players, coach Tim Sheens still tore strips off those wearing the lime green jersey. "They were atrocious – simple as that," he said. "The A graders in Canberra tackle better than them. The first possession [Illawarra] had, they scored, and that's just not good enough.

"We've come down but a few people obviously thought that because [the Steelers] had plenty of people out, they were going to be maybe a little bit easier than they thought. But we've had our bums smacked in all three grades. So there are going to be some rude awakenings this week, I can tell you now."

Whatever Sheens did that week must have worked; the next weekend they welcomed the Sharks to Bruce Stadium with a 40-16 thumping. As for the Steelers, the win put them back into the top five, though that position would be under threat the following week when they had to travel to Penrith to face the Premiers.

It was a game where Wishart made it back into the run-on side for the first time that season. It also saw brothers Craig and Brad Izzard face off against each other. It wasn't the first time it happened and, while it would be unlikely centre Brad would come into contact with forward Craig too often, the Steelers captain said there would be no going easy on a sibling. "If he can get a shot on me he'll give it to me and if I can get one on him I'll give it to him as well," Craig said.

Penrith came away with the win at home 24-12, despite the Steelers taking a 10-6 lead at half-time with the help of an eight-point try. Craig Simon, who was making his first grade debut (and his only top grade game in 1992) in the halves next to brother John, had flung a pass to McIndoe to score in the corner.

Penrith's Steve Carter was penalised for some rough stuff after McIndoe touched down, giving Girdler an extra shot from right in front, having already nailed the sideline conversion. Early in the second half, the Panthers retook the lead 12-10 and from there they were never headed. The Steelers could only add a Girdler penalty goal to their halftime score when John Simon was knocked down after putting in a kick ahead.

Ultimately it was the Panthers' big pack with the likes of

Mark Geyer, Paul Dunn and John Cartwright that wore down the young Steelers. But Penrith coach Phil Gould was full of praise for the men in scarlet and white.

"Illawarra played really well. They are a great young club and a great young side. It was an outstanding effort by our club today to win all three grades," he said.

"To outscore those blokes 18-2 in that period [after being behind 10-6] was outstanding. Taking into account that we were behind at half-time, we had a couple of setbacks – an eight-point try and a bloke sinbinned for 10 minutes – to win the second half 18-2 was a great effort."

The loss was tempered by the news that a number of Steelers were picked for representative honours. Wishart, McGregor and John Simon (to replace an injured Ricky Stuart) were all named in the Country Origin side to play on Friday night. "It's an honour to be picked in the Country side," Simon said. "Wollongong is more a country town than part of the city. It's an hour from Sydney and I don't regard myself as a city player."

It marked a return to form for a player who had struggled through the last season with a back injury. Unable to train properly, the weight went on and Simon's form slumped. In the 1992 pre-season he managed to get some relief from the back ailment and trained the house down, resulting in sparkling early season form.

A near certainty for selection earlier in the year, Russell was left out of the Country side, perhaps in part because his two-week suspension left him somewhat short of match fitness. Young forward Cross made the cut for the Country Firsts side.

Around the same time, Queensland named its 30-strong State of Origin squad, which left out Steelers five-eighth and centre Fritz. Murray expressed his disbelief that Queensland couldn't find room for him. "Queensland are specials to win the State of Origin series if Dale isn't in this squad," he said.

"If they've picked 30 players and can't find a place for Dale, then it's a hell of an outfit. They must have a fair side, some very talented backs, because I'd rate him in my top side."

All the Steelers' City-Country reps were chosen to take the field against Manly the following day, though there would be some shuffling done during the week. Cross was picked to start, putting Russell on the bench though Murray changed his mind late in the week.

The home match against Manly was also expected to see the return of captain Walsh from an knee injury suffered in the Round Two win over Cronulla. After having his "cartilage scraped" according to the *Mercury*, Walsh hadn't been able to train. Also the troublesome knee had to be drained just days before the game. That understandably made Walsh very doubtful to start in the eyes of Murray, especially with the Steelers having the following week off due to the State of Origin split round.

"We play Brisbane next and they should have a few in the Origin side so if Chris misses this week he might get a fortnight off."

On paper, the Steelers were favourites for the Anzac Day match (where ex-service personnel would get into Steelers Stadium for free). Manly was coming to town on a three-match losing streak, falling to Penrith, Newcastle and

Brisbane. The game against the Broncos saw Sea Eagles coach Graham Lowe brand it as Manly's worst performance since he'd been at the club. Murray, perhaps remembering the way the Steelers played the Gold Coast like they'd already banked the win, wasn't having any of that.

"I expect them to be a lot different to last week," he said. "They will be all fired up, coming off three losses in a row and looking down the barrel of number four. It's not a matter of being complacent but more of not getting into a false sense of security."

Simon, Wishart and McGregor were fit enough to take the field at the showground the day after Country's 17-10 win – the first since the 1987 introduction of the 'origin' rule allowed NSWRL players from the sticks to be picked for Country.

Simon admitted to a low-key preparation for the Manly game – he got home from City-Country at midnight, watched some MTV, went to bed and slept in the following morning. Though he might have pushed the bounds of believability a little too much when he told the *Mercury* "I had a few cans of soft drink after the game, then off home."

Captain Izzard almost missed the Manly game after waking up on match day with a slipped disc. "I felt pretty crook when I was driving to the game and thought I might not be able to play," he said. "I talked Graham into letting me have a half an hour's physio and it worked."

Despite Murray's efforts to avoid a false sense of security, the Steelers found themselves down 10-2 in the shadows of half-time from a try to Darrell Williams and three goals to Michael O'Connor. But the Steelers players didn't wait until a half-time spray from Murray to fight back. Minutes from the break a scrum packed five metres from the Manly line. The Steelers won it and Simon flung the ball to Fritz, who gave it to McGregor to do a little bit of magic. Sliding across the defensive line, Mary suddenly stepped, beating one defender and drawing two others. Girdler, who had by now figured support play was where the tries were to be had, loomed up along McGregor's left to cross the line. The young centre guided the ball between the stick for a 10-8 scoreline.

Girdler then equalised right on half-time thanks to one of the most obvious offside tackles you'll ever see. Girdler set up the play, passing to an unmarked McIndoe who pinned his ears back and raced to the line only to be pulled up a few metres short. A quick play the ball saw it end up in the hands of Russell a few metres out from the post and a shot Manly defence in front of him. That was when Des Hasler, who was still trying to make it onside from the McIndoe break, chose to tackle Russell, instantly giving away a penalty and 10 minutes in the bin. Girdler took the easy two points to level the game at 10-all at halftime.

"If there was any luck on offer in the first half, Manly seemed to collect it," Murray said after the match. "When we came up with 10-all at halftime, I was pretty happy. I thought maybe some of the luck might start to go our way.

"You do have to make your own luck and there's the effort that you have to put in when you really want it. Our fellows really wanted it."

The Steelers continued the momentum in the second half, scoring 13 points while holding Manly scoreless. In the process, Girdler nabbed another double with a try that was a carbon copy of his effort in the first half. It was his third double for the season and, coupled with his five goals gave the teenager an individual points haul of 18 for the match.

Despite it being his first season in the top grade Girdler knew enough not to big-note himself, instead giving the tryscoring credit to his team-mates. "The other blokes are just making a habit of putting me in for them," he said. "I just put the ball over the line. That's the easiest part of it. I'm happy to do that if they keep setting me up."

One player didn't remember much of the Steelers comeback win. Fullback Riolo was smashed high in a tackle by Williams in the first half. The *Mercury*'s back page photo showed a clearly concussed Riolo being held up by trainer Dave Stanbury as he was helped from the field. In an era where concussion didn't rule a player out, Riolo later returned to the field but what happened out there was a mystery to him.

"I don't remember much about the game at all," he said. "I don't really remember the tackle or who made it. There was just heaps of blood."

On top of the whack across the face, the Manly game saw Riolo diagnosed with a stress fracture in his foot. The injury wasn't caused in the game, but something he had suffered without knowing for some time; the result of a stiff foot that restricted movement though he fought through it before it was diagnosed.

"I've done a lot of running and it's never been affected," he said. "If it was just a matter of the fracture healing I would be okay. The main thing is now we know what is causing it,

I have to make sure my foot is loose before coming back. Otherwise I would be back on then back off again."

That effort to get the injury right would take longer than anyone expected; Riolo ended up not playing again until Round 18 – missing 12 matches. All that time off the field was something the fullback found hard to deal with.

"People are good, they ask you how you are. But there's the bad side. You get sick of talking about your foot. It just makes you depressed."

13

While the Steelers had the following week off due to the split round, several members still had a game to play. Wishart and McGregor were picked for the NSW Origin side. It was the first sky blue jersey for the centre, which came as a bit of a surprise because he'd only played three matches that season due to injury.

Getting a late call-up was Simon, brought into the side to shadow Ricky Stuart who was still suffering the effects of the injury that left him out of the City-Country match. "I'm not exactly sure what the situation is but it doesn't worry me whether I actually play or not," Simon said. "Being selected in the Country origin side was honour enough.

"The selectors have basically stuck with proven players, so I never really thought much about being picked for NSW. Now I'm happy to train as part of the team and see what happens."

What happened was Stuart didn't overcome his injury in time, so Simon wore No7 for the Blues in a match won 14-6 by NSW. It was Simon's only Origin game in 1992 and he wouldn't be picked again until 1997. For McGregor, Game

Alive in the Five

One of the 1992 series would be the first of 14 matches for NSW.

Still, the rapid improvement of Simon saw the Steelers move to lock down the half to a long-term deal. Contracted to the end of the 1993 season, the club looked to extend that deal by offering to find him a job as well.

"John will be a pioneer of this sort of thing in our club," Millward said. "I can't give many details but the sort of job we will be offering will give John plenty of time to get out on the training paddock."

The media love a good hoodoo. If a team struggles in a few consecutive games against a rival, that's a hoodoo. If a team has never won at a certain ground, that's a hoodoo too. The reality behind those stats don't matter a jot. And so some of the coverage leading into the Steelers' trip up to Lang Park to face the Broncos focused on the fact the Illawarra side had never won at Lang Park.

While strictly true, it was also meaningless. The Broncos had only come into the comp four years earlier so it wasn't as though the two teams had been playing each other for decades. As for not winning at Lang Park, when the Steelers went north in for Round Seven in 1992, they'd only played at that venue twice – in 1989 and 1990. Losing two games is hardly signs of hoodoo.

Perhaps of more relevance was the recent form of the two teams. The Steelers had won their last two match-ups with the Broncos – the Tooheys Challenge and a 19-2 win at Wollongong in Round 14 last season (their first win over the Broncos since they came into the comp). What was impressive about those last two starts was that a team with the attacking might of the Broncos were kept tryless in both games.

Rodwell had recovered from his elbow injury but with McGregor and Girdler carving them up, the headgeared one had to be content with playing in reserves (if you've always wondered what the story was behind the headgear, Rodwell had worn it after suffering a bad head knock in a 1988 Presidents Cup playoff). The much-hoped for return of Walsh, however, didn't come pass. The extra week of recuperation due to the split round didn't result in a fit Walsh.

"It's taken Chris a lot longer to come back from the injury than what was first thought," Murray said. "I'm not putting any pressure on him to come back before he's totally right. As soon as he knows that he is right to play he'll let me know and he'll be put into one of the teams."

That Sunday in May, the Steelers broke that non-existent Lang Park hoodoo. They didn't hold their tryline intact; Alan Cann barged over late in the first half. But that was the only try they scored in the 10-8 win to the Steelers – the only time all year the eventual premiers (who would score 506 points at an average of 23 per game) would be held to single figures. Yes, the Broncos had a number of players backing up from Origin the previous Wednesday, but the Steelers had three players who fit that same bill, so the rep fixture didn't mitigate against the Steelers' win.

The visitors did have a bit of luck, especially in the lead-up to their first try. Just inside the Broncos half, Russell hit the line and threw a crazy overhead, no-look pass to

Docherty – he must have called for it – and the fullback went racing through a yawning gap.

For some reason when he got to Julian O'Neill playing in the last line of defence, Docherty jumped up into him as though he was competing for a non-existent bomb. Maybe wondering what the hell he did that for, while still airborne Docherty flung a desperate pass in the vicinity of some scarlet and white jerseys, but it fell right at the feet of Broncos No6 Kevin Walters who luckily for the Steelers knocked back while trying to pick it up. McGregor, having over-run Docherty's pass, found himself in the perfect spot to pick up Walters' tap back and then strolled over the tryline a few metres away.

Cross got the Steelers' second try via some special work from Simon. Fritz poked his head through the Brisbane line and got an offload away to Simon. The new Blue stepped left, stepped right and then chipped over the head of replacement fullback Paul Hauff as a trio of Steelers raced to the ball. Cross won and planted it down near the posts.

Really, the 10-8 scoreline flattered the Broncos – though the *Mercury* headline "Steelers bury Broncos" was gilding the lily quite a bit. The Steelers made a number of breaks that should have led to tries but were cruelled by a forward pass or a dropped ball. And the Illawarra defence had the home side well contained.

There was a surprising face in the Steelers shed after the game – former Queensland Origin referee Barry Gomersall. The Grasshopper was a hero north of the border while hated in NSW for the falsely-held belief that he tended to favour Maroons.

Sporting a scarlet and white tie, Gomersall had been working for the Steelers as a scout in central and northern Queensland. The connection with the Steelers was that he was Fritz's cousin.

"It started in Moranbah about three or four years ago," Gomersall told the *Mercury* about the background of working with the Steelers. "As you know, Fritzie is from Moranbah. The guys up there were looking around at Illawarra and [the Steelers] said that if ever you're interested, give us a bell.

"A couple of years ago Neil [Lovett, Steelers operations manager] gave me a phone call and that's how it started. I said 'mate, I'd love to be on your recruitment staff'.

"Kids deserve a chance these days and they deserve to go to a club that'd going to look after them. I believe Illawarra has got what it takes to look after the juniors of the future."

While the Western Suburbs ended the 1990s in ignominy; 1999 wooden spooners who won just three games and scored just 285 points all season, the early 1990s were better. The Magpies made the finals in 1991 (after winning a playoff for fifth spot) and would be there again at the pointy end of the 1992 season.

So a meeting with the men in black in Round Eight wasn't going to be an easy game. Both teams had won four games – the Steelers were higher up the ladder by virtue of their first round draw – and were on a two-match winning streak against decent opponents. But a Steelers win was by no mean a certainty.

Yet the Steelers went through the Magpies, winning 17-2

in what was Wests' lowest score throughout the regular season. The Steelers ran in three tries, Girdler kicked two from five and Russell had a "why the hell not?" moment and potted a field goal late. Tryscoring teen Girdler crossed the stripe yet again, but the top try of the match came from replacement Cross sporting a now unusually high jersey number of 40.

He got the ball 10 metres on the Steelers side of halfway and then ran straight through the middle of the Wests defensive line without a hand being laid on him. That's no sporting hyperbole; seriously, there was a gap around five metres wide smack in the middle of the field. Cross used his surprising pace for a backrower to get through the gap before it closed (though the lack of interest shown by Wests defenders suggests he could have walked and still made it through). Then he stepped fullback Shaun Devine playing a shallow cover defence role and pinned his ears back for a 40-odd metre run to the line. Winger Darren Willis was in pursuit and chewing up the metres but could only reach Cross just as he got to the line.

It was such a strong performance from the Steelers that Wests coach Warren Ryan reckoned they'd be there late in the season when the whips were cracking. "On that performance the Steelers are a good thing for the five, in fact they could even threaten for the comp," Wok said. "If they get there, they'll be very hard to beat, and it looks like they're going to get there."

It was also good enough for Murray to adjust his own views of the Steelers' finals chance from something he thought could happen to something he believed would.

Though he didn't adjust the view of his forward pack, especially Gallagher, Billy Dunn, Steve Waddell and David Walsh, who he still felt got no respect from pundits right from the Tooheys Challenge.

"Every side we came up against – Parramatta, Souths, Cronulla, Brisbane – all the way along they kept saying these sides were tough," Murray said. "Souths is tougher this year, Cronulla belted Manly last week, they're a tough bunch of forwards. The week after, we played the Broncos and everyone said they're lot tougher this year.

"None of these [Steeler] forwards got a wrap. So I'm giving them a wrap. I've seen then put their bodies on the line and knocking blokes around."

The Wests match marked the return of Rodwell from injury, playing what was just his second game of the season. "It's a good feeling to be playing again," he said in the sheds after the game. "I'm really happy as I'd been on a bit of a downer for six weeks or so. It's been pretty hard and one of the most frustrating years I've experienced."

Watching from the sidelines he couldn't help but notice how tough the competition for the two centre spots would be, with McGregor and Girdler playing at a high level.

"I've still got to put the performances in to stay there and I'm sure when Paul McGregor comes back, I'll be the first one to go with the way Ryan is playing. So I've got to try and play consistently and see what happens after that."

Sitting in a much better position was John Simon. After the Wests match, the final details of his contract extension through to 1995 were nutted out. Both sides were keeping quiet about the details but it was rumoured to worth around

$250,000. "I went into negotiations thinking I was worth a certain amount and the club agreed," Simon said. With the likes of Parramatta and Cronulla sniffing around, the Steelers had to work quickly to lock up their halfback.

There was no mention of Millward's earlier promise to find Simon a job (though with that paycheque, maybe Simon didn't need a job). Instead, Millward said, it was a contract with a provision for the fast-approaching era of the full-time footballer. "This will enable the Illawarra club to have its major signings available for promotions, training and match-day preparation at any time," he said.

The win over Wests pushed the Steelers up to third place on the ladder, took the club's home-ground winning run to 14 matches and placed them on a three-match winning streak. With the club never before winning four games in a row, it put a strong focus on the arrival of St George the following week.

The Dragons were always going to be a hard ask. After winning four straight games from Round 2-5, they went into a three-week losing slump leading into the Illawarra match. So the Dragons were fairly itching for a win.

"Beating Illawarra down there is a huge ask but certainly not beyond this team," Dragons coach Brian Smith said. "We are the number one attacking side in the competition, which puts us in good stead, providing we pick up our defensive work."

Sitting in the stands to watch, injured Steelers captains Walsh and Izzard got worried as soon as the Dragons ran out onto the showground. The St George side looked as though they'd come to Wollongong on a mission. And that they did, killing off the Steelers' shot of four wins on the trot and ending the home game winning streak with a 21-8 defeat of the home side. Dragons captain Mick Beattie said they'd prepared themselves all week to win.

"After three losses where we scored the same number of tries as the opposition everyone decided to have a go," he said. "There wasn't much talk in the dressing room about Illawarra's record of 14 home wins; nothing much about how they were going for the first four consecutive wins in the club's history. We reckoned Illawarra would play like favourites and make mistakes – and they did."

For a guy who said there wasn't much talk about the Steelers' win streaks, Beattie sure seemed to be aware of them.

The match was the first real taste of pressure for the Steelers. Before this match against the Dragons few people barring their own fans felt this team from Wollongong could be a serious competition threat. But going into Round Nine, people knew the Steelers were the real deal. That, combined with the knowledge of the pair of winning streaks hanging in the balance, perhaps saw the pressure bite down on the Steelers. They made too many uncharacteristic mistakes and turned in their flattest performance of the season to date.

To find a bright spot, there was the return of Piccinelli through reserve grade. Despite having not played a first grade game since August last year, Murray had seen enough of the reserves match to put Piccinelli on the bench for first grade, where he got on as a replacement in the 60th minute.

With the Steelers stinging from having their winning streaks brought to an end, in Round 10 they were presented with a chance to do the same to someone else. South Sydney were on a three-match streak at their "home" ground of the Sydney Football Stadium, that cavernous venue that was always way too big for a regular NSWRL match. That three-match streak was misleading as to the Bunnies' overall form; they'd only won one other game that season and lost five placing them in 10th spot.

A loss to the Steelers would create a less-than-wanted streak for the Bunnies. From the start of the season, they won and lost in pairs; defeated in the first two games, they won the next two, lost the two after that and got the W for the next pair. With a last-round loss to the Broncos, a Steelers win would continue that odd pattern.

And that pattern did indeed continue, once the Steelers lifted their game in the second half. They went into the sheds 6-6 after a try to Cross that came one tackle after Russell put Simon through a gap, racing 30 metres but getting tackled when he couldn't find any support. Souths' six points came via three penalty goals to winger Eion Crossan.

In the second stanza, the Steelers put on another 11 points while keeping Souths scoreless (and their tryline intact). Girdler didn't find the tryline in the match, but Simon did, via some heads-up play by Piccinelli, who came on in the second half. He was tackled just in Souths territory and played the ball to Schifilliti, who took a dart from dummy half only to get grabbed by the defence. Rather than clock off after the play the ball, Piccinelli backed up and got the pass from his hooker and broke through the defence before offloading to a trailing Simon who scored next to the posts.

The Steelers came away with the two points, consolidating

their place in the top five. But that flat first half, where several scoring chances were bombed, did raise a few concerns for the team's consistency. And consistency would be what was needed if they were to make the finals.

14

It's hard to understand how anyone thought the format of the post-war British Lions tours was a good idea. In the years after World War II, the English came here and spent more than two months playing any side that put its hand up. At least that's how it seemed. At times the visitors played 20 or more matches.

Some of those were the Tests against Australia, obviously. But there was also a load of games against local rep sides – NSW, Queensland, Ipswich, Toowoomba, Darwin, Wide Bay, Monaro and Riverina. While the locals no doubt enjoyed trying to match it with the pride of English rugby league, the Brits must have been absolutely buggered by the end of it.

One of those regions that was on the itinerary right through to the late 1970s was the Illawarra – though the team was variously known as South Coast and Southern Division before some bright spark realised there was enough talent in the Illawarra to justify its own rep side. Between 1946 and 1979, the locals played the Brits nine times with the chocolates being evenly divided. Both sides won four games with one ending in a draw. It wasn't until the Lions' fourth post-war tour in 1958 that they beat the southern reps. However, from 1970 onwards, the Brits certainly had the wood on the Illawarra, winning the last three rep fixtures.

That 1970 match at the showground was the most spiteful of affairs, with the visitors winning 24-11. One Illawarra League official said "it was the dirtiest game I have seen". Seven Southern Division players had to be treated by doctors after the match. Fullback John Air had his jaw broken after copping repeated head-high tackles – missing six weeks for club side Thirroul.

"The Englishmen we have known down here on earlier tours were gentlemen," Air told the *Mercury*. "I would not say the same of this side. The Englishmen tackled around the head all the time, and there were always two or three of them in each tackle."

Collegians halfback Jim Matthews had a broken cheekbone and Shellharbour's John Armstrong a gash over a swollen eye that required 12 stitches and his other eye was black. At least four other players ended up with stitches for head wounds.

"It was the worst injured team I have seen in my life," said strapper Les Griffin. "I have had to work on them most of last night and today. When rugby league comes to this it is grim."

The Illawarra rep side lost the chance to play the British after the 1979 tour because, by the time they came back in 1984, the Illawarra Steelers existed. Through the 1980s it was unusual for a NSWRL club to take the field against the Brits. That changed in a big way on the 1992 tour where the

Steelers, Eels, Seagulls, Raiders and Knights all got a crack at the tourists – and only Parramatta could beat them.

The Raiders didn't care much for the game – an absurd effort at scheduling meant they played the Lions the night before an afternoon match against Parramatta. So the Raiders thought "bugger that" and as well as the compulsory resting of their four Test players, a further five First Graders had a break. Playing at Bruce Stadium in the middle of winter, the English must have felt right at home, winning 24-12.

Newcastle took the match more seriously than any other club; with only Test player Paul Harragon missing out. Fat lot of good it did; the English walloped them 22-0. For anyone who cares, the Seagulls went down 28-10. Parramatta had a decent side on the field for their 22-16 win, though the big story from the match was the 100-metre foot race between Martin Offiah and Eels winger Lee Oudenryn. The Parramatta player was the clear winner; though there were rumours Offiah tanked on purpose because his team-mates bet on Oudenryn after the odds were too good to resist.

The other club game on that tour was the Monday, June 8 match against the Steelers at the showground, just three days after their match against Souths. Fortunately the Great Britain match fell during the Queen's Birthday long weekend, so no-one in the 10,021-strong crowd had to chuck a sickie to be there.

Cross was rewarded for his reliability and effort by being named captain of the side. He had taken on the leadership role in lower grade sides, both at the Steelers and state footy, but this was the first time he had the C next to his name for a top grade fixture. "It was a bit of a shock," he said. "Being chosen to captain the Steelers in this match is definitely the biggest thrill of my career. It's a once in a lifetime chance – to play the Poms."

It was the sixth match of the tour for the British Lions (though that included several matches in Papua New Guinea and a game against the Queensland Residents – one could argue they were expected to win all of those). While Canberra didn't care about the game, the Steelers did, putting a decent team on the park. Though not their best – there was no Wishart, McIndoe, Simon, Rodwell, Fritz or Riolo. In their place would be the likes of Jonathan Britten, Aaron Whittaker and Wests signing Michael Neil getting his first-run-on start of the season.

The British team taking the field knew the first Test was coming up later that week and, with a few spots up for grabs, they were keen to prove to coach Malcolm Reilly that they should be picked. That made for an at-times torrid encounter, where both forward packs bashed the crap out of each other.

British winger Graeme Hallas got the scoreboard operators working via a stunning 75-metre try in the 12th minute. Casually fielding a kick on his own 22, he turned and raced up the touchline, breaking through three Steelers tackles before planting the ball in the corner.

Six minutes later and Girdler (of course it was Girdler, who else would it be?) picked up a four-pointer with the help of some luck. Neil put in a short kick five metres from the line, which rebounded off a Lions player's legs. Girdler toed the ball into the in-goal and touched down. With he and the

Lions kicker missing the conversions, the score sat at 4-all.

Minutes before halftime halfback Shaun Edwards crossed to take a 10-4 lead into the break. Eight minutes into the second half, perhaps sensing this was going to be a defence-heavy match, Kevin Ellis potted a field goal, which would be the last time the Lion troubled the scorers. But it was a one-pointer that would prove crucial.

The Steelers had their chances to trouble those scorers too, but too much dropped ball and errant passes cruelled their fortunes. It wasn't until the 71st minute that the Steelers got their next point, via a try to Whittaker. It came on the back of a long series of tackles in the British quarter, which sparked the crowd chant of "Steelers! Steelers!" in the hope their team could scrounge up a win. But the home side had left their run too late.

Reilly was magnanimous in victory, noting the Steelers had taken the game down to the wire. "The Steelers turned up the steam and made it pretty hot for us," he said. "They controlled the ball a lot better in that period [late in the game] and we had to scramble."

Murray, aware that the game had no bearing on the standings on the league ladder, chose to overlook the team's handling errors – at least publicly. "They were playing against the 30 best players in Great Britain and some them are in the top 13, so I reckon it was a great effort."

Thanks to the split round, the Steelers had a week off to rest up after playing such a rough defensive match.

15

It took less than a minute to work out the Bulldogs' game plan in the Round 11 match at the showground. They were going all-in on what is euphemistically referred to as "spoiling tactics", but really tends to mean "cheap shots". Just 48 seconds in, Dogs five-eighth Terry Lamb and a teammate went in to tackle Brett Docherty. The fullback left the field in a daze, his arms around training staff's shoulders, blood streaming from his face.

That led to a backline reshuffle, McGregor coming on as Rodwell's centre partner, Girdler moving to the wing and O'Meara taking Docherty's fullback spot. But Lamb wasn't done. In the fifth minute ref David Manson cautioned him for a high tackle on Russell. The incident was captured by the *Mercury*, which ran it on the front page – it looks like an old-fashioned coat-hanger. But Lamb stayed on the field (not even being binned for a professional foul with the Steelers in a scoring position). Manson seemed to let the Dogs get away with a bit, so much so that it led to Schifilliti getting into a punch-up with Simon Gillies over some rough stuff in the ruck.

"The Steelers hung in grimly as Canterbury cynically hammered and spoiled its way to the lead in the first 40 minutes," wrote the *Mercury*'s Mike Gandon, "never allowing Illawarra to get into stride."

The Dogs took an 8-4 lead into the break and it wasn't until ringleader Lamb left the field with a calf injury that the Steelers began to climb back into the match. That started from the most unlikely of sources, a kick from forward Steve Waddell. Bulldogs fullback Ewan McGrady failed to clean up and O'Meara touched down with Girdler slotting the conversion from the sideline.

"Muzza [Graham Murray] says it's always a good option on the fifth just to put a grubber in rather than be caught with the ball," Waddell said of his deft kick. "It was the fifth tackle, I just put it through and the opportunity came up. It picked everyone up and we just had to hang on then in defence and it worked out well."

Waddell's reference to "hanging on in defence" suggests a close game, but from that try in the 56th minute the Steelers were the only side who scored. They eventually ran out winners 24-8. After the game the Steelers promised to review the tape of the tackle that knocked out Docherty but little came of it. Lamb was free to take the field the following week against Cronulla. Docherty was less fortunate, missing the next two matches. As the results would indicate, they were good matches to miss.

In the lead-up to the North Sydney Oval match against the Bears, the Illawarra was being ravaged by a flu virus. "Thousands of men, women and children in the Illawarra and South Coast are already stricken with the virus which appears to be spreading through communities like wildfire," the *Mercury* reported.

There were Steelers players among those thousands, including star centre McGregor. His illness was deemed significant enough to make the front page of the *Mercury*. McGregor said he was sick when he played in the Canterbury game.

"I only went on the field because I am so attached to the Steelers and they needed me," McGregor said. "I thought I might have it for a few days and then recover quickly. But that hasn't happened. It just won't go away."

McGregor ended up playing against the Bears; given the lethargic performance from the Steelers, one could suspect a number of other players were also suffering with the flu. In a game Murray described as "boring" Norths won 11-4, with Daryl Halligan's three-from-four being the difference in a match were both sides scored one try each.

"Predictable football bordering on boring became the order of the afternoon," the *Mercury* reported, "in front of 8309 hardy souls who had to endure a match where a negative, uncompromising, unfashionable style dominated even the slightest attempt to open up the game."

In a case of understatement, Murray said it wasn't the best game the Steelers had played. "We were looking for someone to ignite us, but just couldn't come up with it. We knew they were going to run from dummy half and play it pretty tight. It was boring. We were looking for a couple of breaks to go our way."

In his mid-week column for the *Mercury*, Murray went a bit further, saying the Steelers had to play better if they wanted to be there at the back end of the season.

"As hard as it is to admit, Illawarra has to pick its act up or face troubled times in the race for a semi-final position," he said. "We never got into stride against the Bears, who are becoming renowned for sticking to a basic pattern and wearing down their opposition."

Still in the top five, it created a bit of pressure for the next game against Balmain, who were looking to bounce back from a three-match losing streak. "The Tigers enjoy throwing the ball about and we'll have to be on our guard to counter their attack," Murray said.

There was a boost of good fortune going into that game, with Piccinelli named in the starting line-up for the first time in 1992. Murray had been impressed with his efforts in reserve grade and coming off the bench in Firsts – including tries against St George and Canterbury. It wasn't good fortune for Gallagher, who had to step aside to make room.

"As I explained to Dave Gallagher I wasn't unhappy with what he's been doing," Murray said. "It's just that in some cases the fellow behind them is playing that well that he forces himself into the side. That's what Neil's done."

Piccinelli's return wasn't enough to lift the Steelers, who crashed to a 22-12 loss after getting back into the game just after half-time via a try set up by fullback O'Meara. Fielding a Ben Elias kick, he scythed through the Tigers defence before sending McIndoe away to score.

But overall it was a game that found the Steelers out of sorts; making mistakes, things falling apart in attack, missing tackles. Behaviour that was more like the Steelers of old, rather than the 1992 version. Schifilliti especially saw it; when he was replaced late in the second half, he was expecting to be in reserves the following week. "I went to training prepared for the worst," he said mid-week. "My form hasn't been up to scratch for about four weeks now so if I'd been dropped it wouldn't have been any surprise."

He wasn't left out of the side to play Parramatta, Murray declining to go into panic mode just yet, not even with the Steelers sitting on third, just one win away from a logjam of teams in fourth.

"I wouldn't say that it's a crisis situation. We've got to clean our act up and come to terms with our situation. We've got a game against Parramatta next week and we will be looking to break that streak."

Murray did change up a few things to freshen up the team. He opted not to make the team sit through a video session of the Balmain game, instead holding a team meeting where he set a target of winning the remaining five home games. He also staggered training sessions, rather than running them around on consecutive nights. The second night of training was cut short so the team could bond over dinner and a few drinks.

It relieved the tension – as did Girdler placing a cockroach on Waddell's meal. "We knew it was plastic because Crossie picked it up and ate it," Murray said. "That broke things up and we got back to what we were before, instead of worrying about things."

The team was given some extra motivation, the chance to win for Chris Walsh, who had announced his retirement in the days before the Parramatta game, having struggled to get back to fitness after an injury suffered against the Seagulls in

Round Two.

He'd been trying for months to make the return to the field because he'd overcome serious injuries before. In 1987, he broke his neck against the Dragons, when a tackler forced his head down onto his chest. Despite feeling tingling and numbness in his arms and getting a number of X-rays, he kept playing over the next three weeks and then collapsed in the sheds after the game. That was when the docs found the two fractured vertebrae in his neck. The docs told him his playing days were over, but Walsh knew different. He worked to strengthen his neck and was back on the field in 1988. "I don't know if you forget the pain when you've been out of the game or not," he said, "but I really want to get back into it."

And he did that in spades, winning the club medal in 1988 and 1989 and captaining the Steelers in the Panasonic Cup final. In 1991, injury cut short his season again, this time via an ankle injury that required the insertion of a screw.

He came back for the 1992 season, injuring his knee in the Tooheys Challenge match against the Bunnies. Walsh battled through it for a few weeks but had to give up the Gold Coast match when his knee started locking up. "So I went for an arthroscope and found that I had both cartilages torn, also a lot of wear and tear in the joints," he said. "I had my medial cartilage out, my lateral cartilage trimmed up and some other work done in there."

After that he was in the pool swimming laps, riding on exercise bikes and doing weights in an effort to get back on the field. But the knee wouldn't co-operate, getting to the stage where he couldn't run without pain. That was when he got another arthroscope and the specialist discovered his knee was bone on bone.

"I was waiting for the knee to come on. It didn't respond – if anything it got worse," Walsh said. "I'm pretty disappointed with the way things ended up. I would have liked to go out playing. The fact that in the last two years I haven't played a great deal is pretty disappointing and very disappointing for the club too, I suppose."

Now on top of the urgent need to stop a losing streak, the Steelers had the added motivation of winning one for the skipper. Though the Steelers were a little slow to get going against the Eels, who were second-last on the ladder. At half-time the score was just 2-all. Murray wasn't too worried; unlike the Tigers game, he could see his players had plenty of energy left. They used that energy to full effect in the second half, running in four tries – including a double to Bill Dunn – to run out 24-2 winners.

"I was watching them [the Eels] last week on tape and got that feeling that you've got to chip away at them," Murray said. "They're not a mug side. I thought going into the second half at two-all, just the way we kicked and chased and kept the pressure on them, that maybe they were going to crack – and they did."

But it wasn't a story about the Steelers' return to form that made the front page of Monday's *Mercury*. On page one was a photo of a knocked-out O'Meara lifted onto a stretcher after being hit high by Eels fullback Scott Mahon in just the sixth minute. The *Mercury* made it perfectly obvious where they stood; the headline over the image read "Stop this thuggery".

"Eleven thousand people saw a young footballer smashed senseless in a blatant act of thuggery at Steelers Stadium on Saturday night," the story read. "The referee paid to control the game apparently did not.

"As a result 20-year-old Steelers winger Brendan O'Meara was carried from the ground on a stretcher, officials fearing he may have a broken neck after a jarring head-high tackle."

O'Meara's neck wasn't broken; he'd be back on the field the following weekend. The crowd booed ref Kelvin Jeffes who, after having stern words to Mahon, decided he could stay on the field for the rest of the game. But he also awarded the Steelers a penalty, which suggested Mahon had broken the rules – just not bad enough to be sent off. Despite the fact an opponent was being carried off in a stretcher.

Mahon had form in this area; in a Round Seven match against the Dogs he copped four weeks for a high tackle. The Steelers game was only Mahon's third back from that suspension. The league judiciary didn't take as lenient an approach as Jeffes, suspending Mahon for eight weeks – which would take him to the end of the 1992 season.

Judiciary member Ron Coote warned Mahon to fix up his game or find some other sport to play. "This is the second time you have been here for a desperate attempt and it ends up a careless tackle," Coote said. "I think you will have to change your technique if you want a future in rugby league."

16

In what was becoming a weekly event for Murray, the Steelers line-up had to be rejigged following prop Craig Teitzel dislocating his shoulder against Parramatta. The initial prognosis wasn't good; the giant was expected to be out for six weeks. That would end up being eight, he didn't make it back in the side until the first week of the finals.

David Walsh was brought up from the bench into the starting line-up, with Izzard becoming the new fresh reserve. McIndoe too was sidelined with a shoulder injury, giving the rookie Pauls his fourth start of the season (Pauls may have been a good luck charm for the Steelers; in the six matches he played in 1992, the team won five of them. The only loss would be to the finals-primed Broncos in the last round).

The round 15 clash against Easts wasn't going to be a problem. The Roosters were coming in off the back of a three-match losing streak while the Steelers were riding high after that demolition of the Eels. The Steelers took the Sydney Football Stadium match 18-6. McGregor was back to his best form, setting up two tries, for Simon and Cross. That first came with a bit of luck; McGregor made a break down the right-hand side of the field and was looking for supporting team-mate. There was one there, but he was covered, so instead McGregor threw the ball into open space to the team-mate's left.

At first it looked like a pass gone wrong and the play was about to break down. But then it became clear what had happened. Simon had called for the pass, and McGregor threw it into the gap to let the half grab the ball on the bounce and score.

There was the potential for drama going on in the background to this match. Murray had started negotiations with the club for a new deal. The day before the Friday night clash with Easts, the Steelers board told him they'd made no decision on an offer to retain him. It was an amateurish effort, given Murray had the team sitting second on the ladder on eight wins after Round 14. Hell, the Steelers had five *seasons* where they couldn't win that many games. Re-signing Murray should have been a no-brainer – and a priority.

Perhaps the board were too focused on the pipe dream of signing Canberra Raider Bradley Clyde, who was off-contract and entertaining offers. A realist could tell Clyde was never going to leave Canberra, though the Steelers may have devoted more attention to wooing the Raider than trying to keep hold of what they already had.

What Murray did in response was put the pressure on the board, going public with his dissatisfaction after the win over Easts. The board, holding the totally reasonable fear a rival club would steal Murray away, met on Saturday to come up with a deal.

The two-year deal was reported to be worth $100,000 a season, with Murray signing the following Friday. "I'm glad this is over and done with so I can now focus all my attention to the team, and the Newcastle game in particular," Murray said.

The coach wasn't the only re-signing worry that surfaced the week of the home match against Newcastle. An unknown at the start of the season, Girdler had started every game so far this season and his tryscoring ability, support play and goalkicking saw the teen chased by as many as six rival clubs.

In the previous two matches, Girder had been pushed out of his preferred position of centre to the wing, Murray preferring the pairing of McGregor and Rodwell. It gave Girdler a taste of what could be his lot in the coming weeks, that despite his stunning rookie season so far, he might be the loser when the Steelers had a full-strength side.

"My aim is to play first grade now I've had a taste," he said. "I don't want to be a fringe player and I think it will be hard for me to hold a spot when Rod Wishart and Alan McIndoe come back from injury. "If other clubs are after me to play first grade I'm happy to do that, while here I could be used as a gap player."

Earlier in the season, the board said they didn't let escape those players they wanted to keep. Girdler would prove to be a big test of that statement. McIndoe too was coming off-contract, though the winger was looking at retirement due to work commitments rather than packing up and moving to another club.

"We have made an offer to Alan which we believe is very fair and deep down I think Alan thinks it is too," said Steelers operation manager Neil Lovett. "Alan must make a decision between his work and the club – there is no doubt that if he plays football next year he will play with us."

The match against the Knights was going to be much more of a challenge than the coasting effort against Easts. Newcastle were in the top five and, like the Steelers, shaping as 1992 finalists. Murray knew the side would have to lift from what he had called the "sluggish" and "lethargic" effort against Easts.

"As I explained to the boys, we've had a bit of a social week," he said after the Easts game.

"We played on the Saturday, went out afterwards, backed up on Sunday to swim with the [Wollongong] Whales] and had a sponsor's do on Monday. So, I guess, without making excuses for them, they were a bit low-key tonight.

"But now that's it for the season, let's get our heads down now and we'll get back and be a bit more enthusiastic next week."

Murray didn't want his side to get caught up in a forward battle with the Knights' big boppers, which would be playing into Newcastle's hands. Instead, he wanted to see the ball go out wide, where the form centre pairing of Rodwell and McGregor could go to work.

"I expect Newcastle to play it in tight with their strong pack, but there may be something for our centres to exploit out wide," Murray said.

That Knights forward pack would be without its leader in Harragon. In his first ever appearance before the judiciary, the Chief was suspended for three weeks over a high tackle in the previous round that left Norths' David Fairleigh with a broken nose. Desperate for their prop to play, the Knights lodged an appeal on Friday afternoon. They were hoping for a hearing on Friday night or the Saturday morning, but the league said it was too late and that no appeal would be held until Monday.

In the lead-up to the Steelers-Knights clash, Channel 9 delivered an extraordinary snub. The network's Sunday night TV game wouldn't be the match-up between the two teams tied for second spot. Instead the TV slot would go to the Raiders-Panthers match, teams sitting ninth and sixth on the ladder and who would both finish a long way from the top five in 1992. It was a suggestion that the network figured teams in regional areas just didn't rate, though anyone could see the Steelers match was the game of the weekend.

"This match involves the two equal-second teams, with the winner going to outright second and the loser probably going back to fifth spot and in jeopardy of missing out on the semi-finals," Millward said. "So it is certainly a crunch game."

It was Channel 9's loss; the network missed a tight game where the home side took the win 8-6. The Steelers had to come from behind, down 6-2 at half-time. Murray threw Piccinelli on the field for the second half and the rangy second-rower soon went to work. He made a break and lined up McGregor for a pass. Once Rodwell saw Mary had the ball, he loomed up in support and strode away for a try, converted by Girdler.

From there the Steelers mounted a strong defensive effort, knuckling down when McIndoe was sinbinned for the last 10 minutes. With the game on the line, the players inspired each other with calls of "Dubbo", a reference to the defending that won them the Tooheys Challenge.

"We call it Dubbo from when we had a tough game out at Dubbo," Fritz said. "It's to try and remind us to keep going, to keep scrambling because they made a real lot of breaks in that last 10.

"It's the way we want to be playing – to try and come up with a win when we're down a player like that, especially against a side that was coming second."

17

The 1992 season was one that saw the slow but constant move towards full-time players. The Steelers could afford to offer the likes of Simon a contract that would mean he didn't have to work, but many of his team-mates had full-time jobs to juggle along with the increasing commitments of first grade football.

A team-mate perhaps in the worst position was second-rower Craig Izzard. Living in the western Sydney suburb of Erskine Park, Izzard was a police officer working the night shift. In the lead-up to the 8-6 win over Newcastle, Izzard had worked from 11pm on Saturday to 7am on Sunday, then headed home for a while before jumping in the car for the drive down to Steelers Stadium. After the game, there were muted celebrations for Izzard; he had to go home and try and get some rest before heading off to work at 11pm that night.

"It affects my energy level and gets you in the second half more than anything," Izzard said. "It's alright in the first half but once you start getting a bit tired it starts to affect you then."

Alive in the Five

On training nights, Izzard also had to drive down to Wollongong, stopping to pick up Penrith boy Steve Waddell and Campbelltown locals Brett Docherty and Dave Gallagher. Despite all the travelling and impost on his time, Izzard chose to shelve plans to quit at the end of the season.

"I was troubled by a back injury last year at Balmain and I was thinking about giving it away after 1992," he said. "But now I'm talking to the Steelers about a new contract. Not only is the side going well but my form is showing the benefits of me being injury-free. That's something to keep playing for."

For the second time in the 1992 season, the Steelers were on the verge of setting a new winning streak record. Between Round 6 and 8, they racked up three wins, giving them the chance to win four in a row for the first time in the club's history. That milestone wasn't reached; they fell to the Dragons.

They had another shot at the record going into the Round 17 match against the Sharks, after wins over Parramatta, Easts and Newcastle. In his preparation, Murray had to work hard to ensure his charges didn't look at the ladder, see the Sharks sitting in equal last spot with the Gold Coast and figure it would be an easy win.

He highlighted the way the Sharks played the previous weekend against the Broncos, who had led the competition since round 12. "Cronulla was unlucky last weekend," Murray said. "Looking back, they probably should have won. It was 16-6 to Cronulla but it could have easily been 20-6, and the score could have been anything. Even towards the end they still had a chance to win it and did everything they could but just couldn't get over the tryline."

There was also the fact that the Steelers' second place on the ladder was fragile. With tiny margins separating each team in the top five, and a number of others sitting just one win out of that select group, one loss could result in a very big fall.

"We only beat Newcastle by two points, but they went from equal second to fifth," Murray said. "The realisation is that if you don't win or keep winning you can drop very quickly."

Sadly, the team didn't appear to heed those warnings. The lowly Sharks beat the second-placed Steelers 10-6, a scoreline that flattered the visitors somewhat because they only got on the board in the final minute via a Simon try. As Murray warned, the Steelers fell down the ladder to fourth. It also meant the chance for that four-game winning streak was lost again. (For the record, the Steelers would finally get that four-match winning streak the following season).

"We had some frustrated footballers," Murray said. "Things weren't going our way and we made errors. We've got five games to go and we've got to put our heads down and get back into winning mode."

Coincidentally, the following week's game was against the other cellar dweller the Gold Coast Seagulls who had won just five games so far that season. After being ambushed by the Sharks, it was paramount that history didn't repeat itself.

The team's chances got a huge boost with the

announcement that Wishart would be suiting up for the home game against the Seagulls. Ongoing hamstring problems had meant Wishart hadn't played a club game since Round 7. Having only played four games for the club in 1992 he had earned a nickname from team-mates that the *Mercury* said "cannot be repeated in a family newspaper" (the likely sobriquet was "tampon", the usual insult for a regularly injured player – "in one week and out for three").

'It's been really frustrating playing only four games for the Steelers," Wishart said. "I've played more representative games than club games. When you look at it, it doesn't look good. But that's the way it's turned out. Nothing's better than running out for Illawarra, especially at Steelers Stadium."

While out injured Wishart had sought treatment from Sydney doctor Neil Halpin, who performed manipulative surgery on Wishart's hamstrings. "Hopefully he won't have any further troubles," Halpin said. "In the past the injury has never properly healed. There would be a build-up of scar tissue in the leg and when he really stretched out the muscle would tear. That's why he keeps aggravating the injury."

Wishart's return meant Shane Wilson lost the wing spot – he would only play one more game in the 1992 season, a bench start in the Round 21 last-gasp win over the Sea Eagles in Round 21.

The Steelers played themselves back into a bit of form against the Gold Coast, running in seven tries in a 36-14 thumping. It was the second-highest score an opponent racked up against the hapless Gold Coast that season – only surpassed by Newcastle's 42-6 flogging. Rodwell racked up a double, and Wishart crossed the stripe in his first game back.

But the *Mercury*'s league writer Mike Gandon was concerned the magnitude of the win might paper over some worrying cracks. "It would be folly to go into next Sunday's match against Canberra at Bruce Stadium with a false sense of security," Gandon wrote.

"This is because of some flimsy defensive lapses on both sides yesterday, although a number of unforced errors from the Seagulls were generally punished to the limit by the much hungrier Steelers attack."

It turned out to be a very prescient observation, because that match against the Raiders would make the Steelers finals hopes seem very shaky. And Murray, who had so far avoided reaching for the panic button following a loss, had little option but to send a few players down to reserve grade. Especially when two stars made headlines for all the wrong reasons.

18

If someone was taken to Bruce Stadium on the afternoon of Sunday, August 9, to see their first ever game of league and they were asked to pick which team was heading for the finals, they would have guessed wrong. The Raiders – the team that lost three on the trot and had been out of the finals race for weeks – absolutely beat the crap out of the Steelers to the tune of 38-2.

Brett Mullins scored a double, the lime green machine ran in six tries in total and David Furner had the radar boots on, kicking seven from seven. The Steelers? A lone penalty goal just before half-time. The Raiders' motivation was posted on their dressing room wall. A sign referred back to the team's dismal outing at Wollongong earlier in the season. Under the heading of "Illawarra" it read "first grade – loss by 29 points; second grade – loss by 18 points; 21s – loss by 28 points; total – 75 points".

Those 38 points scored by Canberra were the most a side racked up against the Steelers in 1992. And you had to go back to 1989 to find the last game they leaked more points, a 44-8 scoreline – ironically against the Raiders. Even the

Steelers' hometown paper couldn't sugarcoat the abject thumping Illawarra received, branding the performance as "abysmal".

The only saving grace for the Steelers was that the three teams below them in a very tight race for the top five – St George, Wests and Newcastle – all lost on the weekend. It stopped the Steelers paying dearly for the shellacking by falling out of the top five.

The loss meant the Steelers' finals aspirations were on a knife's edge. With three rounds to go, the Steelers had to win two of them to guarantee a place in the finals. There were no easybeats in those last three opponents. First up was defending premiers Penrith, still with an outside chance of the finals. Then it was a trip to Brookvale – where the Steelers had never won, having played there eight times since 1982. The Sea Eagles were in the logjam of teams sitting just outside the top five. The last round was against the Broncos, who were looking like certainties for the premiership.

Somehow Murray managed to keep his cool when talking to the media after the debacle he'd just witnessed, resisting the urge to pour scorn on his players.

"We were certainly beaten comprehensively," Murray said after the game. "It's back to training and business as usual, but we've got to come up with some answers. We'll have a good look at the video and dissect it and then we'll just have to do better next week."

Instead, he kept his powder dry until after the team had gotten back to Wollongong. Two days after the thumping at the hands of the Raiders, Murray pulled out the razor and cut six players out of the starting line-up. O'Meara made way for

McIndoe, Schifilliti was called back up at the expense of Dean Callaway. Hardworking forwards Cross, Piccinelli and Walsh were dumped for Russell, Gallagher and Bill Dunn.

The most high-profile axing was Simon in a big fall from grace given he'd made his Origin debut earlier that year. "He's been struggling to find form in first grade for the past couple of weeks," Steelers operations manager Neil Lovett said. "John's at that stage now where he will very quickly find his form in second grade and could still play a major role in the end-of-season matches should we qualify for the finals series."

In his place would be Balmain signing Mick Neil, making the Steelers' run-on side for the first competition game that season (though he had taken the field for the match against Britain). "Neil has been playing impressively in second grade and has been used several times as a replacement player in the past few weeks," Lovett said. "He's got experience in end-of-season matches, having played in grand finals for Balmain."

Also not helping the team preparation for a crucial match against Penrith was the news that two Steelers – Russell and Girdler – had been involved in a brawl at Waves nightclub two days before the loss to Canberra. In a front page story, the *Mercury* reported a woman at the Towradgi club complained to security she had been "showered with beer". Security then began escorting Girdler out the door, when Russell decided to step in.

"The security staff said a scuffle followed," the *Mercury* reported. "One security guard alleged he was struck during the scuffle." The police were called, and the security guard initially decided not to press charges because he didn't want to ruin the players' careers. He changed his mind when one of them – the report doesn't state which one – became abusive – and then changed it again when they apologised.

With the scuffle happening two days before the Raiders match, it did raise questions about whether it was a factor in the loss. Girdler wasn't named in the side to take on the Raiders, due to a fractured finger he suffered in the Seagulls match. But Russell was supposed to be nursing a neck injury – and a nightclub scuffle is not the best way to take care of that. As it was, the morning after the incident, Russell withdrew from the side to play Canberra due to the injury.

It saw some thinking Russell had actually injured his neck in the scuffle, something which Millward denied, noting he had injured it the previous week against the Gold Coast. "Ian had a neck injury all of last week and was receiving physiotherapy for it," Millward said. "I couldn't say whether it [Russell's withdrawal from the team because of injury] was related to the Friday night incident."

Girdler was in the news that week for another reason as well. The teenage rookie – who had fielded offers from Easts, Canterbury and Penrith – decided to sign with the Panthers. The team's leading pointscorer – and fourth across the whole competition – had been the biggest beneficiary of the Steelers' high injury toll. He was rushed into first grade after Rodwell was injured in the Tooheys Challenge and did what every replacement player should do – make it impossible for the coach to drop him. He stayed in the side even after Rodwell was fit, Murray choosing to find a place for him on the wing rather than leave him out of the side.

Alive in the Five

Also, the hamstring troubles of regular kicker Wishart saw Girdler become the team's first-choice kicker.

It wasn't so much an issue of money that saw Girder leave but a dislike of being shunted out onto the wing. His preferred position was centre and he realised his chances there were limited with McGregor and Rodwell forming the strongest centre partnership in the competition. Two months of negotiations between the club and the local junior couldn't find a way around that impasse. Millward felt that no team would guarantee a player a walk-up start in any position.

If Girdler figured that was what the Panthers were offering, he wasn't quite correct. Penrith also signed Cronulla veteran centre Mark McGaw for the 1992 season, which blocked Girdler's path to his desired spot. He ended up waiting seven rounds before playing his first game for the Panthers, but once he got that centre position he kept it all season.

Docherty was also looking for a new club, saying he was not impressed the Steelers hadn't even bothered to talk to him. "I'm disillusioned with Illawarra at the moment," Docherty said. "They haven't even approached me about next year and Balmain have. I have to weigh up my options and while I'll give Illawarra the last option I can't wait around forever."

Docherty ended up signing with Easts rather than Balmain. He only played one match for the tri-colours – coming off the bench against the Steelers. From there he signed with the Western Reds and helped develop the game on the west coast, though he never played a first grade game for the Reds.

Neither Girdler or Docherty played in the Round 20 Penrith match at Steelers Stadium. Girdler was coming back from that fractured finger (though sceptics would wonder if it was actually punishment for the Waves incident). As for Docherty, with Riolo back in the run-on side since the Raiders match, it would turn out he had already played his last top grade game for the Steelers in Round 18 against the Gold Coast.

The Steelers relieved some of the top-five pressure with an 16-2 Round 20 win over the Panthers, half Neil turning in a match-winning performance, where the Steelers led 14-2 at the break.

Murray was pleased the Steelers had put the huge loss to the Raiders a week ago behind them. "You can go one of two ways," Murray said of the Steelers' return to the winners list. "If we had been beaten by 20 today then I would have some doubts. But to come back like today and stick it to them and come up with the points shows the character of the side."

However, the win over Penrith came at a cost. After sparking the Steelers attack in the first half, Russell collapsed six minutes into the second stanza after a seemingly innocuous tackle on Paul Dunn. In agony Russell couldn't rise to his feet and ended up being stretchered off the field. The initial fear was that he'd torn his hamstring, but later checks suggested it wasn't that serious, leading to hopes he'd be back for the finals.

But he wouldn't. The injury was worse than first thought; he had torn the hamstring off the bone, and bone fragments had come away as well. Russell had played his last game of 1992 for the Steelers, which certainly affected the team's

Alive in the Five

chances of success in the finals

19

Years later, even knowing the result of the Steelers clash with Manly at Brookvale, watching the game back makes you think you got it wrong. Maybe they didn't actually win this game, you think. Because with the clock ticking down, and the Steelers behind, it really looks like they're toast, like there is just no earthly way they could win this game.

And yet they did.

While the Steelers had to win one of their last two matches to seal a top-three spot, the reality was they had to beat Manly in the second-last round. Leaving it all on a last-round defeat of Brisbane was a fool's gamble. The Broncos had lost just one game since Round 11; they were definitely not a side you wanted to face in a must-win fixture.

Ahead of the Sea Eagles game, there was a slight financial distraction – were the Steelers to beat Manly and lock in a finals berth, the league would pay the club $100,000. For a side like the Steelers, where ready cash was not as plentiful as at other clubs, that would have been a very welcome windfall.

But Murray was not worrying about that – or having the focus on the semi-finals. "We need to concentrate on the match itself," he said. "It's not actually winning the game to make the semi-finals, it's winning the game to beat Manly."

And Manly weren't going to be easy. As well as the Brookvale hoodoo to overcome, the Sea Eagles were on the cusp of the top five. A win over the Steelers and a last-round victory over the Sharks could have been enough to see Manly squeak into the finals. On top of that, there was the sentimental element; it was Michael O'Connor's last game at Brookvale. The star centre had come to Manly from St George in 1987 and stayed for six seasons, just in time to be a part of their 1987 premiership. There was a push from fans to send O'Connor out a winner in his last home game, and the 18,294 crowd figure for the game was the second-biggest at Brookvale that season. The Steelers had all that to overcome. And they left it until the last minute to do so.

In the 17th minute, the Steelers took the lead following a bit of luck. On the last tackle attacking the Manly line, a defender knocked a Neil pass back 10 metres, giving the Steelers another set of six. Wishart picked up the loose ball, wound up and barreled into the defence as he did so many times in his career. This time he didn't break through to the other side. From there, he played the ball to Schifilliti and it went left to Neil and then Riolo. Running towards the corner, the fullback threw a pass that cut out Rodwell, finding Piccinelli on the edge. He drew in the centre and winger, offloading to Pauls, who performed an elaborate swan dive to get over the line.

There was measure in Pauls' madness; in an era where the corner post was in play, his getting air robbed scrambling defenders of the chance to smash him into the black-and-white cardboard tube and into touch.

Wishart missed the conversion from the sideline, and the score remained 4-0 through to half-time. The Illawarra side were handling whatever Manly threw at them, though the wheels seemed to be coming off in the shadows of half-time. Pauls fielded a short kick from Lyons and got turned around in the tackle. Disoriented, Pauls got up and played the ball facing the wrong way, turning Manly marker Des Hasler into surrogate dummy half.

In the next set, Manly came within millimetres of scoring via a barnstorming run from John Jones. Riolo's grassing tackle around the legs pulled him down and a desperate lunge from Cross up top stopped Jones from sliding over the tryline.

With the last tackle the next play O'Connor kicked to the in-goal but it went dead. Referee Greg McCallum gave Manly a let-off, penalising the Steelers for being off-side. Captain Schifilliti had a chat to McCallum, which must have been getting rather heated because Waddell had to come over and usher the hooker away.

O'Connor missed the penalty goal and the Steelers brought it back into the field of play. But a touch judge immediately ran onto the field to report Fritz for impeding a Manly player as the five-eighth ran back to offer support for the ball carrier. In what seemed an over-reaction, Fritz got 10 in the bin and Waddell also received a caution for something or other.

This time Ridge took the shot at penalty goal, though he also missed. Minutes later, with a scrum packing down, the half-time siren sounded. Schifilliti, standing right next to

McCallum, took the opportunity to raise a few issues; it was a discussion in which Schifilliti looked increasingly frustrated.

The second half was an about-face from the first; Manly gradually took the ascendency while the Steelers looked like they'd never score. First Craig Hancock touched down from a deft chip kick by Martin Bella (of all people!) but he was ruled offside.

Soon afterwards, Manly made a break for the Steelers' line, only for Piccinelli to snuff it out via a come-from-behind tackle on David O'Donnell. Then came a messy play the ball, with a Steelers player lying in the ruck and Piccinelli nowhere close to being marker. He stepped through, wrapped up the dummy half and McCallum said he could go spend 10 minutes in the sheds. That left the Steelers down to 11 men, with Fritz still off the field. Despite having a numbers advantage, O'Connor directed Ridge to take the penalty shot, moving the scoreline to 4-2.

In the 52nd minute, the Sea Eagles crossed the line courtesy of the man of honour O'Connor. Neil threw a wild pass that Fritz (now back on the field) couldn't pick up. O'Connor toed it through and got one of those room service bounces to scoot away and score under the posts. Manly were now in front 8-4.

While there were still plenty of minutes left, the Steelers were playing uphill and not looking like they had so much as a single point in them. Their only genuine chance came from an attempted intercept by Wishart. With the pass over his head, Wishart got hands on it but couldn't pull the ball in. Had he gotten control he was a virtual certainty to sprint the

60 metres to score.

By the time the clock had reached the 75th minute, Manly decided to play for field position, figuring the game was in the bag. Ray Warren and the other TV commentators were in the same boat, talking about how Manly had kept their finals hopes alive, while the Steelers faced a hard game next week against the Broncos to guarantee a top-three finish. And fair enough too. No-one could have predicted what was about to happen.

It started with what looked like the end for the Steelers. Rodwell was put into touch, which was game over. Well, it would have been if the touchie hadn't told McCallum he was dragged over the line after the tackle had been completed. So from looking like they were about to lose possession right when they needed it to mount a last-minute dig for points, the Steelers got a penalty with a touchfinder seeing them start the last six tackles of the game five metres into Sea Eagles territory.

A bustling run from Dunn put the Steelers 10 metres closer to the line with less than a minute on the clock. And then the miracle play happens. After Simon is tackled after dancing around, trying to create a gap out of nothing, Riolo slotted in at dummy half and threw it right to Neil, who fired it out to Piccinelli, who took the ball to the line.

Then the rangy second rower threw a gem of a pass to Rodwell, steaming into a gap. That the centre actually caught the ball was impressive, because it deflected off O'Connor's hand. Geoff Toovey scrambled over in cover defence. Rodwell waited to draw him in before passing to Wishart less than 10 metres from the line. With only Ridge desperately coming across in defence, Wishart used the fullback's momentum against him, stepping inside and crossing the line.

Then, most likely because he's the kicker, Wishart raced around to put it under the posts as the siren sounds. That move sealed the win for the Steelers. A try brought the score to 8-all; a conversion from the sideline was less of a sure thing than one from right in front of the sticks.

It was a breathtaking finish, one that came completely out of the blue. Not even the man who coached the Steelers expected it, Murray spending the last few minutes of the game thinking about the Broncos. "I suppose you tend to think about next week when it gets like that," he said.

Still, he liked what the last-gasp win showed of his team. "It showed a lot of intangible things – character, sheer guts, club spirit, all those things. You can't train for them. You have to find them in the blokes. And you're never dead until the final siren."

In the visitors sheds, the Steelers celebrated sealing the club's first finals appearance. Over in the home side's shed, the man who only had one more match left in his career was shellshocked. "I can't believe it, I really can't," O'Connor said. "I honestly thought we'd did enough to win the game. It's a … nightmare."

With the Steelers heading to the finals, fans flocked to the side's last home game, against the Broncos. In the days when buying a ticket could only be done in person, people started queuing up from 6am the day after the win over Manly. By lunchtime on that Monday, the club had sold more than 1000 grandstand tickets and 2000 in the concourse.

"It is an unprecedented demand for tickets in the 11 seasons we've been in the competition," Millward said. Despite that surge, the 14,512 crowd for the home game against the Broncos crowd wasn't the biggest of the season. It wasn't even in the top three; matches against St George (17,469) Wests (16,058), Canberra (14,881), Newcastle (14,611) and Penrith (14,586) all pulled in more fans.

Locking in the finals berth also saw the start of a series of colour posters in the *Mercury*, much remembered by fans (this book's title takes its name from one of them). Each one featured a colour photo of a Steelers player along with an inspirational headline. The first featured Paul McGregor with the slogan "Go get 'em Steelers!". Brett Rodwell got a start in the next poster, accompanied by the iconic (from a Wollongong perspective) slogan of "We're alive in the five!".

Then there was the deal offered by the *Mercury* and Caltex servos. Take the full-page newspaper ad into one of those petrol stations and you could score yourself a free Steelers headband – a accessory no football fan has ever asked for.

If the Steelers were to manage to beat the Broncos in the last round, they would have to do it while low on troops. Russell was still out – though some fingers were forlornly crossed that he'd be fit for the finals. Rodwell missed the last-round fixture with a severely bruised toe and McGregor was also on the sidelines due to a leg injury. The casualty ward saw a backline reshuffle; Simon, who had come on late against Manly, was named as the starting No6 along Neil. That pushed Fritz out to the centres, where he paired with Girdler (also back last week – oddly wearing jersey No 50 –

against Manly), with Pauls on the wing replacing the still-injured McIndoe.

Even though both sides were finals-bound, Broncos coach Wayne Bennett didn't figure the match would have anything to do with the post-season. "I don't think this match is of any bearing for what is to come," he said. "Obviously, we're not coming down there to lose, but we have five guys out injured and Illawarra has injury problems too, so you can't read too much into what happens.

"As for the semi-finals it's too far ahead to say Illawarra and Brisbane will be meeting again, so this match can't be seen in a semi-final context."

The game could, however, be looked at in a weirdness context. The Steelers went down 15-8, a fine effort against a side that had scored more than 20 points in 15 games that year. Also, the Steelers led 8-4 at the 64th minute, with the Broncos running in two late tries.

The weirdness came with the nature of the Steelers points tally of a try and two goals. *All* of them were dubious at best. Wishart had a penalty shot from in front which clanged off the left upright and through the posts … maybe. The two touch judges weren't sure, taking some time to raise their flags. Broncos winger Pat Savage certainly didn't think it went through the sticks; he caught the ball and started running it into the field of play. By using geometry one can presume it went between the posts; how else could Savage have caught the ball in-goal? But even after numerous replays of the match coverage it's hard to see definitive proof it was a goal.

There's no shadow of doubt in the Steelers' next six points

– a try to Dunn and Wishart's conversion. Both were screw-ups by the officials. Schifilliti put a grubber into the Broncos in-goal. Unbelievably, Dunn is the only one chasing – and no Brisbane players are anywhere in sight. All he has to do it ground the ball and it's a try. But he muffed it, his hand grazing the ball enough to knock it on (Girdler, following on his heels, knocked it on too). Dunn knew he'd screwed it up; there he was lying face-down in the in-goal, his head in his hands.

To try and con the in-goal touch judge, Girdler and Neil started giving Dunn congratulatory pats on the back for scoring – and possibly to stop him from making it so obvious that he hasn't scored. Inexplicably, the in-goal touchie awarded the try, prompting a now-legendary outburst from commentator Paul Vautin, "This bloke at the back here, they should tip him straight out to the sea … Wollongong Ocean or whatever it is out there."

All the while, the camera is focused on the touch judge, whose mannerisms give the clear impression he knew he'd screwed up. Brisbane lock Terry Matterson is so outraged, he gave referee Greg McCallum a spray, earning him 10 minutes in the bin.

Next up it was the touch judges' turn to mess it up. Wishart was awarded the conversion, despite replays clearly showing the ball passing outside the left-hand upright.

The NSWRL responded by saying neither the touch judges or in-goal judge would get any work in the finals. With Brisbane getting the rub of the green the previous week when Kevin Walters awarded a try despite knocking on, the league started making noises about using video replays to help the ref.

"I would concede that it's now going to have to be seriously looked at," league chief Ken Arthurson said. "While it would be financially prohibitive to do it in every game, I suppose we're going to have to discuss the possibility of us using it during the finals series."

Major Preliminary Semi-final
Illawarra Steelers vs St George Dragons
Sunday, September 6, 1992

In Sydney, finals fever is limited to a few suburbs linked to that successful team. When the finals came around for the Steelers, it was a bit different in Wollongong – the whole city got behind the team. Those *Mercury* player posters were tacked up in the windows of houses and on the walls of shops.

As well as a Schifilliti poster calling "Let's Do It Steelers!" the first week of the finals saw the now legendary Rod Wishart poster, complete with the clumsy but cute phase "Our Ro(a)d To Glory". Apparently no-one at the paper thought of "In Rod We Trust". Sigh.

Scarlet and white colours were everywhere. The 400 kids at Barrack Heights Public School got to wear the Steelers jerseys to school and office staff at banks across the city had tellers sporting freshly-made "Steelers 1992" T-shirts. Even those headbands launched by the *Mercury* and Caltex that

Alive in the Five

now seemed so lame were a hit. They burned through the initial order of 10,000 in less than a week and had to rush in more. "People have been wearing the headbands on hats," *Mercury* marketing manager Glenys Holby said, "tying them to car aerials, etc and even wearing them in shops and to work."

Superfan Pat Went made the front page of the paper with an eerie prediction for the first finals match against St George. "My heart is going boom, boom, boom already. It's a worry, but I reckon we can win by two points."

Lord Mayor David Campbell donned a Steelers jersey for a photo, though it didn't seem to be a cynical move designed to hitch his wagon to the Steelers popularity train. Campbell had been following the Steelers that year; he and wife Edna had booked tickets on a small plane to fly to Dubbo for the Tooheys Challenge at the start of the season. A casual fan doesn't go to that sort of effort.

Also in the week of the preliminary semi an unexpected school friendship between Rodwell and Tumbleweed guitarist Lenny Curley was revealed. The muso and the footy player hung out in the same group at Holy Spirit College.

"Brett was a bit of a deviant really," Curley said. "Nothing too bad, just clowning around stuff trying to get away with what we weren't supposed to." Perhaps because he was worried people wouldn't get that Curley was joking, Rodwell noted that you could never take him too seriously.

To help some of those who had just jumped on the Steelers bandwagon, the *Mercury* published the lyrics to Leon Berger's team song *Taste of Steel*. Surprisingly – to me at least – it's more than just a chorus. That's the part with the "gonna give 'em the taste of steel" line that always seems to be the only part of the song that gets played.

But there are actually two verses in the song as well. For the record, here they are;

First verse
We mean it
We're gonna make it happen right
And when the whistle goes
We're gonna get out there and fight
It's our best game
It's our name
It's our red crusade

Second verse
We're gonna shake 'em to the ground
Gonna keep on scoring tries
Gonna keep on winning games
We're out to play
We're out to stay
It's our red crusade.

Millward was pleased, but not surprised by the sudden surge of support for the Steelers. "This has been building for 11 years," a pleased Millward said. "It's to be expected and it's very pleasing and encouraging for the team."

Former coach Hilditch said he knew the Steelers had the potential to make the finals, he could see it coming during his years at the helm. "When I walked out I could see they were about to go ahead in leaps and bounds," he said. "They had the young talent all ready to walk into first grade in a year or two. When I was there, without denigrating the players we had, a lot were players who couldn't get a go at other Sydney clubs and they were just going through the motions."

The *Mercury* even got Millward to name the Steelers best team since they entered the comp in 1992. Not surprisingly, the bulk of the team featured players who were playing finals footy; Wishart and McIndoe on the wings, McGregor and Rodwell in the centres, Simon at No6, Russell at lock, Schifilliti at hooker, with Fritz and Piccinelli on the bench.

The rest of the squad was foundation fullback Dorahy, five-eighth Brian Hetherington, second-rowers Wayne Springhall and Geoff Selby and front-rowers Chris Walsh and Mark Broadhurst. The other two bench players were Rod Reddy and Andy Gregory.

Amid all the scarlet-and-white fever a story about the struggles of Wishart struck a sombre note. While he had been dealing with injuries that kept him off the playing field, they paled in comparison to what else he'd been dealing with.

In January of the previous year, Wishart's younger brother Derek died after an asthma attack at footy training. Then in July this year, a close friend of his sister Kirsty was murdered in her house. Kim Corrigan was shot dead in the kitchen of her Kiama home. The Wishart clan extended the hand of friendship to her husband Brian. "Publicly, and whenever we were in their company," Wishart said, "they were the perfect couple, so seemingly happy and devoted to each other."

That vision became clouded when Corrigan was charged with the murder of his pregnant wife. The following year

Corrigan, who initially claimed an intruder had shot Kim before changing his story to claim 'voices in his head' made him do it, was sentenced to 22 years in jail.

Finally just a month before the finals, the driver of a car died when they collided with a truck on the Kiama bends. Behind the wheel of the car was Carmel Wishart, the wife of Rod's brother Cliff.

The week of the finals Wishart chose to speak about what helped him through these tragedies – his Anglican faith. "I simply believe that God has a plan for everybody and I adopted that attitude after my brother Derek died," he told *Mercury* editor Peter Cullen. "My Anglican faith and that attitude helped me pull through."

In terms of preparation for the Illawarra side's first finals game, Murray had to yet again take injuries into account. Not only would Russell be out for this game – and indeed for the entire finals series – the Steelers would be without defensive five-eighth Fritz, who broke his hand a few tackles into the last-round match against Brisbane. "I hurt it really early in the match. I tried to do my best but I was falling off tackles and unable to do a lot of things. There was a lot of clicking in the hand and it was painful so I had no alternative but to come off at halftime."

Watching Fritz in that Brisbane match, it's unclear just when he sustained the injury, but it's obvious it affected his defence. He can be seen grasping and grabbing players with his left hand, doing his best to avoid having to call on his injured right hand.

It meant the Steelers were heading into the finals without

two of their best players.

Also in doubt was Izzard, who broke his wrist three weeks earlier against Penrith and hadn't played since. Looking for any solution, Murray booked Izzard in to see legendary boxing trainer Johnny Lewis at his gym in Newtown. Having trained Jeff Fenech – who had suffered hand injuries throughout his career – Lewis had become the go-to man when dealing with such problems.

"Johnny had me catching basketballs," Izzard said, "and it felt pretty good. With a needle and strapping I reckon I will be alright to play." He would indeed, though Murray wisely used the still-sore Izzard as a bench player rather than a starter.

On the upside, the Steelers had their first-choice backline in place for only the second time this season in fullback Riolo, Wishart and McIndoe on the wings and McGregor – who had missed the two previous games with injury – and Rodwell in the centres. The only other time those five were in the run-on side was the Round 20 match against Penrith. That was clear evidence of the relentless injury toll the Steelers had to deal with in 1992.

Simon took over Fritz's No6 jersey, pairing with the experienced Neil. Murray felt that would help Simon; an organising halfback in his playing days, the coach had been looking for that in Simon. Realising the young player wasn't there yet, he switched him to five-eighth where he could just play what he saw, and left the planning up to Neil.

The Steelers and Dragons had only met once in the regular season, in Round Nine and the Illawarra side copped a 21-8 drubbing at home. In that game, the big Dragons pack dominated and Murray was expecting to see more of the same.

"I expect the Saints to play exactly the same way they did back in May," he told the *Mercury*. "We've shaped up a number of times in the forwards this year when we needed to. We made too many mistakes in our own quarter."

On game day the Sydney Football Stadium was packed. With the Steelers' scarlet and white looking very similar to the Dragons' red and white, it was hard to tell whose supporters dominated, though the Steelers club had loaded up at least eight buses full of fans to the game.

The Dragons were the first out onto the grass. "This is the team most fancy to play Brisbane in the grand final," Warren said on the TV commentary. It wasn't an outrageous claim; the Dragons had finished three points clear of the Steelers on the ladder and had won eight of their last nine games. The Red V warmed up on the field while waiting for the Steelers to appear, captain Schifilliti leading them out of the tunnel. The players faces bore a mix of awe and focus; they looked like a team who felt they were ready but also fighting a bout of nerves at being on this strange new stage.

"Now Illawarra comes out," Warren said, " for the biggest occasion in rugby league – their first semi-final. Some people say it can't be done, but a Cinderella story could easily unfold in 1992."

The team had an extra spark at the SFS. Prowling the sidelines would be the welcome sight of Stanley the Steel Avenger. That week there had been concerns expressed in some corners that the Steelers would be the only team in the finals without someone dressed in a mascot suit running up and down the touchline. The team used to have someone wearing the Stanley suit a few years ago, but he had moved interstate and the club hadn't been able to coax anyone else to do the job.

"We ordered a new model in May," Millward said a few days before the match against the Dragons. "We paid a half deposit and the artwork was great. It was supposed to be ready to introduce to the public for the game against Great Britain in June but it didn't arrive.

"We are still in dispute with the production people. We're still trying to finalise something for the finals, but I can't make any promises." Perhaps it was the public shaming, but somehow the Stanley suit arrived in time for the first finals match.

Simon kicked off for the Steelers and the arm wrestle through the forwards began. The Dragons had the better of it; by the time each set drew to a close, they were far enough downfield that a kick from either Brad Mackay or Mick Potter landed near the Steelers' goal-line.

After just three minutes that field position paid off for the Dragons. Still inside their own quarter on the last tackle, the ball went back to Simon – alone in the backfield – to get a kick away. Dragons hooker Wayne Collins got in his face a charged down the kick. Unfortunately for the Steelers the ball didn't ricochet over the sideline but behind Simon, where there was no other Steelers player.

Collins chased the rolling ball and was on his own when he picked it up and dove over in the corner to score what was his first try of the season. "You've really got to criticise

Illawarra," commentator Paul Vautin said. "Normally when a long pass is thrown back, there is one to cover the other person. On that occasion, Simon was on his pat malone and that's why the try was scored."

Winger Ian Herron had the kick to convert from the sideline. He went through his kicking routine, which is still unusual despite all the various quirks we've seen from goalkickers over the years. He took his six steps back, then three big ones to the side, turned his back slightly and took another two steps. It was a routine that left him with his back to the goalposts, forcing him to look at them over his shoulder before starting his run-up.

All those steps didn't help him much, Herron sprayed the conversion to the left of the sticks. Still the Dragons were up 4-0. Not too long later, it was almost 8-0. The Steelers got their first decent attacking chance via a Tony Priddle dropball on his quarter-line. In the set, Schifilliti chanced a long pass over to Herron's side of the field and the winger got his hands on the ball and came within a whisker of pulling in the intercept. With nothing but daylight in front of him, he would have been a decent chance of running it in for a try.

Soon after that, the Steelers started to settle their nerves and stop playing stupid football. It paid off not long afterwards, in the ninth minute, when Piccinelli got an offload away despite the attention of several Dragons. Schifilliti took the pass and found a gap in the line. With only Potter to beat, instead of taking him on, the hooker found McIndoe – unmarked after Walford had gone infield to help with the Piccinelli tackle – had come off his wing and was running a cross line. He passed and the winger scored untouched near the posts, Stanley the Steeler leaping in the air in the background.

Wishart took the easy two points on offer via the conversion near the posts, and the Steelers were in front on the scoreboard. "Tremendous fightback so quickly by the Illawarra side," Warren said. "They were playing catch-up football it looked like but there was no need for it. They had been showing nerves in the opening minutes of the game."

Later a scrum packed on the Steelers quarter after a Cross fumble. Ivan Henjak swung the ball to Mark Coyne, who stepped Rodwell so badly that the centre fell over. Coyne made for the tryline only to be tackled by the cover defence. He got a pass away to an unmarked Walford, but McIndoe had come in slightly and managed to intercept the pass before being pushed into his in-goal. It was a lucky break for the Steelers, and great work from McIndoe. Without his effort, the Dragons would have certainly scored.

In the 21st minute, the Dragons did score, but it was only two points and not four. Back in the 1990s, the marker was allowed to try and rake the ball back with his feet. Schifilliti tried that but got pinged by Annesley for not being square at marker. With the penalty within kicking range for Herron, he went through his extended routine before guiding it between the posts. That took the score to 6-all.

After that both sides had a chance to score. Potter – who had trialled for the Steelers but was told he wasn't good enough for the top grade – dropped the ball after Priddle had put him into a gap with a try a possibility. On the Steelers side, Wishart came inside on a scrum play and found a yawning gap in the defence and only Peter Coyne pulling him down from behind 30 metres from the line saved a try. The next play it sailed out to Rodwell, who beat Walford (who was having a shocker of a game) and looked set to score in the corner. Again it was Peter Coyne to the rescue, hitting Rodwell with a shoulder (back when such things were legal) and knocking the ball loose. With the benefit of hindsight, Rodwell may have chosen to dive for the line, rather than staying upright and making himself a bigger target.

Just before the 30th minute Wishart missed a penalty shot that probably still gives him nightmares. Annesley ruled the Dragons inside the five, right in front of the posts. It should be an easy kick for a man who had kicked in the Test arena, but somehow the winger managed to spray it outside the right-hand upright.

Later a brilliant piece of play by Piccinelli almost got the Steelers ahead before halftime. With minutes to go, the second rower took on the unhappy Walford, who tried to wrap him up. Somehow – and it takes several replays to work out just what Piccinelli did – he pulled Walford closer in the tackle with his left hand, then his ball-carrying arm reached around Walford's back and flung a perfect pass to a steaming McIndoe.

With fullback Potter coming in cover defence, McIndoe chose to kick ahead rather than try and beat his opponent. The kick was too strong and beat both attacker and defender over the dead ball line.

"I hope, Rabs, those sorts of opportunities – the missed goal from in front, the try – don't come back to haunt them in the second half," Vautin said in the commentary, "because St George is a good side. They're very consistent this year and they finished very well in their games."

As if to prove Vautin wrong, just minutes after those words, the Steelers laid on a try. With a minute to go before the break, David Walsh offloaded in a tackle to Neil, who threw a wayward pass on the halfway. With the defence rushing up, Cross opted not take hold of the bouncing ball, instead surprising the Dragons by tapping it up into the arms of Rodwell. The centre uses the defence's forward momentum against them, easily making it past Walford's inept attempt at tackle. Rodwell carried it to just outside the quarter, where he drew Potter and fired off a pass to the unmarked McIndoe, who raced off to the corner to score his second try. Wishart made no mistake with the kick this time and the Steelers went into the sheds up 12-6.

Despite being in front on the scoreboard, the Steelers were far from home. The Dragons had come from behind several times during the season, and the Steelers themselves had been known for lapses in defence and attack that let the opposition back in.

One of those very things almost happened in the first set of six after the break. On the last tackle deep in their own half, the Illawarra side bungled the kick downfield, throwing panicked passes hoping to find someone who could punt it. The ball hit the deck and the Dragons toed it through with a try a possibility, but luckily for the Steelers a double knock-on was called.

"That is actually crazy play by the Illawarra team," Sterling said. "On the last tackle you just want to hand the ball over if you can't get a kick away. That's not semi-final football."

After the next 20 minutes passed with no change to the

scoreline, Sterling suggested the Steelers should be looking for a field goal to put themselves more than a converted try in front. The Steelers did better than that; Waddell offloaded to Neil inside the Dragons quarter, who took a step past the rushing defence to find McGregor charging into a gap. Some neat stepping saw him place the ball next to the posts. The jubilant team celebrations in the in-goal make it clear the Steelers figured that was the game.

But at 18-6 down, the Saints started marching in. In the 68th minute, Priddle threw an around-the-back pass similar to Piccinelli's in the first half. Priddle found Herron down the wing, who stepped Riolo to score. With the winger missing the conversion, the scoreline closed to 18-10. That missed conversion would become crucial.

Three minutes later, the Dragons found themselves just over the half on the last tackle. Priddle put in what seemed like an ineffective chip kick – until Potter picked it up and quickly offloaded to Walford on the wing. He dummied, which held up Cross in cover defence just enough to gain 10 metres, before throwing a one-handed basketball hook over the tackling Cross to find Mick Beattie. The centre crossed over near the corner but managed to improve the position for Herron.

Suddenly, the Dragons looked like they were running downhill while the Steelers were looking at the clock, willing full-time to hurry up. There were just seven minutes on the clock when Herron kicked the conversion but, with the Dragons having just raced in two tries in three minutes, a last-gasp win looked a real possibility.

Especially after a Henjak kick into the in-goal threatened

Alive in the Five

to trap Riolo with just three minutes on the clock. The fullback managed to beat Walford's tackle and lunged over the line to get the ball into the field of play. From the Dragons muscled up, the Steelers making just 10 metres by the fifth tackle. Neil almost dropped a poor pass from dummy half, the rushing defence killing off the chance of a kick. There was the chance the Steelers could hand over the ball right on their line, but Neil stepped the runner and offloaded to McGregor.

Suddenly, there was space. The Dragons had been playing a compressed defensive line and, when McGregor got the ball, Herron was the only defender on the left-hand side of the field. McGregor stepped Herron, made 30 metres and then found Wishart running inside the cover defence. Wishart then passed to Neil, who dropped the ball on the halfway. The half slammed the ball to the earth in frustration, though there was plenty of cover defence that would have cut him down well before the line. And they gave the ball back to the Dragons on halfway, further than if Neil had gotten his kick away five metres from the tryline.

From there the Steelers should have simply played field position; get through their tackles and then kick it downfield. But with the full-time siren itching to go and the Steelers inside the Dragons half on the last, Simon inexplicably puts in an attacking grubber, as though the Illawarra side is two points behind, not two in front. Luckily, Simon and not a Dragon, regathered the ball and passed to Walsh. The prop got eight metres from the line before being tackled. Knowing it was the last, Walsh passed off the ground rather than taking the tackle, giving a penalty to the Dragons.

Really, the play was to put it in the in-goal, rather than Simon risking the Dragons picking up that grubber kick and having another shot at closing that two-point gap on the scoreline.

When the final siren sounded, the Steelers players didn't jump around in jubilation. The subdued reaction could be read a number of ways; relief that the game ended before the Dragons scored again, a belief this was only the start and they had more work to do, or a recognition that perhaps they just got away with that win.

After the game Murray could joke about the way the Steelers lost an 18-6 lead, saying his team just wanted to keep the crowd happy. "They were 12 down and needed to come up with quick points. And they did. We didn't need to at that stage but fortunately enough we hung in there."

But reading between the lines, it was clear Murray noticed how close the Steelers came to dropping their first ever finals match.

Major Semi-final
Illawarra Steelers vs Brisbane Broncos
Sunday, September 13, 1992

The win over the Dragons set up another meeting with the Broncos, the fourth that season. The Steelers had the wood on the Broncos, having won two of the three match-ups in 1992 – the Tooheys Challenge final and a Round 7 win at Lang Park. The Brisbane side may have beaten the Steelers at the back end of the season, when form counted for more, but there were still some Broncos wary of the Steelers.

One of those was centre Chris Johns, who worried that Broncos fans were getting ahead of themselves by predicting a grand final berth. "There's plenty of pressure of expectation up here," he said. "While obviously everyone's pretty excited in Newcastle and Wollongong, up here they more or less expect us to go through. Everyone's talking about who we'll be playing in the grand final, rather than whether we'll make it."

Johns was also worried the fans were under-rating their opponent in the major semi-final. "We'll be pretty dirty on ourselves if we lose as well but people seem to forgotten the Steelers have beaten us twice this year. They've got a terrific side and I can't see how we're lay-down miseres by any stretch of the imagination."

Concerns were also raised about a supposed hoodoo at the Sydney Football Stadium – one that was wholly imagined by the *Mercury*. A story in the lead-up to the weekend's match noted the Broncos hadn't played there at all in the 1992 season and that the Maroons Origin side – almost entirely made up of Broncos – hadn't won there in three years.

But the stats showed there was no such hoodoo. The Broncos played at the SFS once in 1991 for one win, five times in 1990 for three victories and a 1989 win in their sole appearance there.

Broncos coach Wayne Bennett was also pouring cold water on the idea of the Steelers being a bogey for his team. That was why he was relieved to beat the Steelers in the last round of the regular season.

"The only thing was to beat them so we didn't have to spend the next two weeks talking about Steelers hoodoos and all that rubbish you guys write about," he told the *Mercury*. "The win meant all that stuff was out the window."

But he wasn't writing off the Steelers, rather he was rushing to their defence saying he was unable to understand why some didn't rate them. To Bennett, there were some similarities to the 1987 Raiders side where he was assistant coach.

"I can't believe the stuff I keep hearing about Illawarra

relying on one or two players or this guy can't play or that guy is too young. I found out all that with Canberra in '87 because when I went there everybody said they couldn't play.

"Illawarra is a lot better football team and has a lot better playing personnel than they get credit for. The similarities between Illawarra and Canberra are amazing – both are under-rated, both have done a lot better than expected and both have a lot of players that are on the verge of becoming household names."

One of those players had already become, if not a household name, at least worthy of being included in the Men of League calendar. The week of the major semi, the calendar was released, with Rod Wishart as Mr July, giving what one *Mercury* scribe referred to as a "come hither" look. "You can't get around it. Don't even try," reporter Julie Beun-Chown gushed. "The fact is that Rod Wishart – Rod the Bod, the Man of Steel, the Hustle with the Muscle – is hot. Sizzling in fact." In an unusual piece of pre-match preparation, Rod the Bod would spend Saturday morning at David Jones signing copies of that photo with his come hither look.

The city continued to show its support for the Steelers, with even fans of rival clubs out of the finals festooning their windows with scarlet and white. Butchers came out with red sausages that turned white when cooked. Letters of good luck flooded into the Steelers Club.

The *Mercury* published a special "Hero-gram" section in its classifieds, where people could pay the paper for the privilege of putting a three-line message in print. The paper also found plenty of fans to talk to. One was the rather large

Corrimal coal truck driver Danny Bock, who wanted a Steelers jersey – he needed a size 60. "I don't think I'm the biggest bloke around but I got the biggest footy jumper," he said. It was so big that when the old Peppers sports store sent the order into Classic Sportswear, they returned a child's size six, convinced the original order was a misprint.

The *Mercury* continued to run those player posters, including one of John Cross bearing the slogan "Australian Iron and Steel". The paper also showed they may have been out of promotions ideas. Readers were offered what was a not-so-impressive supporters pack – made up of a bumper sticker, one red balloon, one white balloon and one red streamer and a white one. People just had to take the ad from the *Mercury* to a Caltex servo to pick one up for free. It's likely the servos were left with a lot of unwanted balloons and streamers on their hands.

That other steel city, Newcastle, was also playing on the weekend – in the knockout match against St George. There were some hoping for a steel cities grand final, including Newcastle Anglican priest Noel Spohr. He'd been calling for divine intervention for weeks, sending a prayer to the heavens each Sunday. "No sense in being half-hearted in praying," he told the *Mercury*. "I'll say one for your Steelers too."

Showing the value of a successful footy team to a city's morale, Newcastle was going through the same supporters' frenzy as Wollongong. "The Newcastle Knights-driven charge to economic and emotional recovery is not unlike that of the Illawarra Steelers," the *Mercury* wrote. "We haven't had an earthquake but unemployment certainly has knocked the stuffing out of us. And like the Knights in Newcastle, the Steelers are giving us something to be proud of."

There was also a sense of hope following from the news that the injured pair of Fritz and Russell were named in the squad to take on the Broncos. Fritz had followed in the footsteps of team-mate Izzard and visited boxing trainer Johnny Lewis for help with his broken hand. After a visit to Lewis, Izzard made it to the bench for the finals win over the Dragons, coming on for two short stints in the second half.

"What I am hoping is for Johnny to say that the strapping will give the hand the strength and the needle will take the pain away," Fritz said. And that's exactly the message Lewis conveyed to coach Murray.

Russell had been improving from the hamstring injury that saw him carried off in a stretcher in the Round 20 match against Penrith. "Ian ran with Graham Murray this morning and again at training tonight," Steelers operations manager Neil Lovett said on the Tuesday before the game. "The improvement in the past few days has been tremendous. Last week he ran with Graham and Graham beat him home comfortably, but this week Ian has turned the tables."

That same night, Murray named the pair on the interchange bench for the Broncos match. But they wouldn't be there on game day; Murray removing them just hours before the match.

There was another piece of bad news for Steelers fans that weekend. In what is unbelievable to a modern audience, the Steelers-Broncos match wouldn't be televised live in the Illawarra. Local fans would have to wait for WIN TV's delayed broadcast at 5.30pm – while Saturday's Dragons-

Knights match would be live.

It wasn't the fault of WIN TV but the result of an agreement with NSWRL, the NSW and Queensland country rugby league bodies and the Nine Network. The deal was restricted to delayed broadcast of Sunday football, because country bodies were concerned it would affect crowds at local matches. The grand final could go out live because those bodies had sent out directives to ensure local finals fixtures were finished before the big game in Sydney.

The farcical ruling overlooked the reality that the Illawarra Carlton Rugby League had moved its final to Saturday to avoid a clash with the Steelers match. It would do the same with its grand final the following week if the Steelers were playing in the final.

Those in the Illawarra who turned on their TV sets for the delayed telecast were greeted with the sight of a 38,000-plus Sydney Football Stadium crowd decked out in scarlet and white. There were surely Broncos fans in the stands but they were hard to find. "They've been doing the Mexican wave, chanting out for their clubs and they're ready for it," Warren said on the commentary.

The Broncos were first to run out, led by Allan Langer. "They won the minor premiership and they won it so easily," Warren said. Then, Stanley the Steel Avenger brought the Steelers out from the sheds into the sunlight of the SFS. "Here they come," Warren said. "One of the Cinderella stories that continues to unfold in this intriguing 1992 Winfield Cup."

While waiting for the Steelers to kick off, one of the TV

cameras focused on Langer. "All the motivation might not stop that little fella from cutting them up if he's on one of those days," Warren said. There was a sense of foreboding from the Steelers about Langer; for whatever reason, the Brisbane half never seemed to be the nemesis to Illawarra that he was for just about every other team in the competition. Would that change now he was on the finals stage, with a grand final berth just 80 minutes away?

In the early stages it didn't look as though Langer – or any other Broncos player – was going to cause a problem for the Steelers. That's because the Illawarra side was dominating. There is an age-old argument about whether a week off in the finals is a good or a bad thing. It will never be answered, but is always brought up when the team with the break has a poor game.

That's how the Broncos started. They didn't look like the side that had lost just two of their last 15 matches, finished six points clear as minor premiers and ran into the finals on the back of a seven-game winning streak. Instead, what they looked like was a nervy team that had scraped into fifth spot and was playing an elimination match.

In the Steelers first set of six Cross put a booming kick downfield on the last tackle, with Brisbane fullback Julian O'Neill bamboozled by the bouncing ball. McIndoe saw a chance to score, picking up his speed, the fullback only just getting to the ball first. The Steelers were on the board a few minutes later via a swinging arm from Alan Cann to the head of John Simon. "Yeah, it's a cheap shot," Sterling said in the commentary, "that fortunately John Simon had half an idea was coming." Wishart converted the penalty goal from in front, though not before Ray Warren reminded viewers of his miss from a similar position a week earlier. The Steelers were 2-0 up in just the fourth minute.

The Broncos still looked sketchy; O'Neill didn't want anything to do with a second Cross kick, winger Michael Hancock dropped the ball 10 metres from his own line. The Steelers were finding gaps in the defence. The Illawarra side was on the board again soon after that Hancock error. The second tackle from the scrum, the ball came out to McGregor who strolled along the defensive line sucking in Broncos before giving the pass for Riolo to score in the corner in the ninth minute. Wishart missed the sideline conversion but the Steelers were up 6-0 and looking like they were running downhill.

But they didn't make the most of that momentum. There were breaks the Steelers needed to capitalise on while their opponents were out of sorts. "You've got to be intense with your defence at all times," Warren said. "The Broncos, they can put a try on you from inside their own 22. Illawarra, they've got to keep up their intensity in defence right through the day."

They soon proved to be quite apt words from Warren. Illawarra fans might have been hoping for something better but it would be another 70 minutes before the Steelers scored another point. In that period, the Broncos went to work, scoring 22 points.

The Queenslanders finally woke up with a sideline run from Steve Renouf. He ran 50 metres but wasn't able to get the ball to Hancock in support. Four minutes later winger Willie Carne made a break down the other touchline, passed it to O'Neill, who found Kevin Walters to put the ball over the line. Kicker Terry Matterson had to wait for the sandboy to realise his presence was needed. Once he was able to build a pile of sand, one of the last goalkickers to walk straight back rather than around the corner and then do a jig, Matterson kicked the two. And just like that, the scores were level.

In the latter section of the first half, the Steelers didn't look as composed as they had earlier. It's as though they'd realised the game had changed. That can be seen in the 31st minute when Simon took the worst field goal attempt you're ever likely to see. It ended up as a grubber kick that went over the deadball line. The game wasn't not even half over and the Steelers were looking for a field goal? That wasn't a sign of confidence in their ability to score more points.

Just a minute before half-time, the Broncos took advantage of the Steelers' shakiness. That danger man Langer got his hands on the ball and stepped his way through a broken defensive line to score under the posts. Matterson put the conversion through and, rather than going into the sheds at 6-all, the Steelers went in 12-6 down. And feeling like suddenly it was the other team who were running downhill.

The second half didn't start well for the Steelers, with Piccinelli not able to return to the field due to a knee injury. Both sides seemed a little flat for the first 10 minutes of the half before the Broncos started to find their way through the Steelers' line. In the 59th minute Langer found some space, stepped Riolo and scored again.

The conversion took the scoreline to 18-6 and the Steelers began to look a bit rattled. "There's just a touch of panic coming into the Illawarra side at the moment," Sterling said. "They've still got 15 minutes to go, there's plenty of time to bridge this gap but it appears as though they want to do it on every play."

That gap got wider in the 68th minute after Langer bounced out of a few tackles and found Carne, who ran 30 metres to score. Matterson missed but the score was 22-6 and it would have taken a miracle for the Steelers to peg back that scoreline. For the first time in 70 minutes, the Steelers managed to score after McGregor somehow avoided being called back for a shepherd before offloading to Rodwell, to send it to Riolo and then Wishart to score in the corner.

Wishart landed the conversion to take the score to 22-12, meaning in the last 70 minutes, the Brisbane side outscored the Steelers 22-6.

The *Mercury*'s back page told the story of the match; "Langer rips the heart out of Illawarra: the headline read. After the game, McGregor noted the damage caused by the guy in the Broncos No7. "Unfortunately we just struck him on a great day. There isn't much you can do to stop him, as today showed."

Captain Schifilliti rued the team's inability to continue the form they'd shown in the opening stanza of the match. "If we can put 80 minutes like our first 20 minutes we will beat any side in the competition by a big margin."

The Broncos' performance in that early period in the game worried Bennett. "For me that was the biggest disappointment of the day," he said. "I don't know why we started so badly but I will have to sort that out."

Coach Murray tried to find something positive to take

away, pointing to the last-minute try. "It was important that we didn't let Brisbane score again and run right away with it," he said. "To score that last try and kick that last goal from the sideline will do a lot for Rod's confidence and for all of us. We can't dwell on this loss."

That would be easier said than done. The Steelers had a chance to qualify for the grand final and they missed it.

Preliminary Final
Illawarra Steelers vs St George Dragons
Sunday, September 20, 1992

The previous weekend had seen the end to the pipe dream of a Steel City grand final. The Broncos had made it through to the big one and, on the other side of the draw, the Knights were knocked out by the Dragons thanks to a 3-2 scoreline. It created an unusual situation where Newcastle found themselves out of the finals despite conceding just five points in their two post-season matches (they'd beaten Wests 21-2 in their other finals match).

The man who had dented the hopes of the Illawarra quickly turned around and admitted he expected to play the Steelers in the big one. "The Steelers never give in, they keep coming at you," Langer said. "That's important in the semi-finals, because although we clicked in the second half, they kept coming at us."

Another throwing their support behind the Steelers was sleeve sponsor MMI. The insurer had actually pioneered the idea of sleeve sponsorship, having to get permission from the NSWRL for the first sponsorship deal in 1998. The new three-year deal – oddly launched at the Sydney Football Stadium rather than the Wollongong showground – was worth around $1 million to the club. "This has been a close relationship between ourselves and the Steelers." said MMI's Wollongong office manager Ian Clifford. "It's been friendly and convivial. I must admit I was a bit hesitant about it in 1989."

With the Steelers now facing a must-win match against St George, Murray was once again worrying about the team's injury toll. Piccinelli had taken a severely bruised lower leg into the Brisbane match, and had only made it worse – which was why he took no part in the second half. McIndoe also took knee and shoulder injuries into the game; they got the better of him 10 minutes from full-time.

Both were felt to be able to take their place in the side on Sunday. It wasn't quite so clearcut for Russell and Fritz, who were both still not at 100 per cent. Despite this, Murray was considering rushing them into the side given the desperate nature of the match.

"They're both 50-50 at this stage for next week, but if they ring me up and tell me they've recovered I'll consider putting them in my starting side," he said. "Then we'd just have to take a look and see who to leave out. Next week is sudden death so I suppose you've got to consider everyone. If you don't put your best side on the field and you get beaten, there's no second chance."

During the week, the focus continued on Russell's hamstrings and Fritz's hand. By the middle of the week, the lock was looking better odds to play in the final than the five-eighth. Murray decided to leave the pair out of the side to take on the Dragons – for the time being. "The option to start Fritz and Russell is there but there is no way they would have been able to prove themselves to me tonight so I left them out," Murray said after Tuesday night's training session. "We'll see how they shape up. It could come right down to lunch-time on Sunday for a decision."

Russell was frustrated at having spent the last five weeks in rehab, working up to the stage where he could manage a jog. "I've been running this week and it feels better," he said. "I've never had a serious injury like this before and it's frustrating to sit and watch your side going so well..

"At this stage I'll be a fresh reserve but I don't want to go into the game and come off after five minutes because I'm not right."

Operations manager Neil Lovett hinted that Fritz wouldn't be happy if injury caused him to miss the final. "He's a tough kid. The hand's broken – he's going to have to be tough to play with it," Lovett said. "It's gonna hurt. But he wouldn't be in first grade if he wasn't tough. Fritzy just won't even consider not playing. He'd rather you punch him in the face than force him to contemplate the idea."

Ending up named on the bench – though likely to be used only in an emergency – Fritz would have to play with the Johnny Lewis strapping and a great big shot of pain-killer. "I've got a six-hour painkilling injection I'll be getting, and I don't think it will hurt at all," Fritz said. "It's just the sight of the needle that scares me." Russell too found himself on the bench, while Piccinelli and McIndoe took their places in the starting line-up.

Also swirling around the week of the big game were efforts to re-sign members of the squad. Neil signed on the dotted line for another two years. "I'm very happy. It's a good club here, the blokes are good and so are the people who support the team," he said. "If I were a young bloke growing up in the Illawarra I'd be even happier. They've got a side of the future."

McIndoe scotched rumours he was going to retire, insisting he had at least another two years in him. "I did approach the club some months ago but they weren't keen to sit down and talk," the winger said. "But I do appreciate them staying away now until the finals are over. They're going to see some risk there with my age, and everyone saying I'm a spent force but I still think I'm playing fairly good football."

Not so happy was forward Dunn, who felt the club was stalling on an extension. "They keep telling me they want to talk to me then put it back, and we haven't agreed on a first-up meeting. It just gets put off week after week. I'm not disgruntled, I'm just tired of waiting for them to finalise things."

Both Dunn and McIndoe would end up going around again for the Steelers in the 1993 season. It would be the last season in scarlet and white for the both of them; McIndoe turned out to have only one good year in him, not two, and by 1994 Dunn was playing for Western Suburbs.

In the hundreds of matches the Steelers played, the 1992 final is the one that sticks in fans' craw the most, the one that conjures up thoughts of "if only" and "what if". It was a game with a low scoreline – just 4-0 via a Ricky Walford try in the corner after the Dragons created an overlap. It was a play the Dragons had tried the previous week against Newcastle but was deemed a failure when hooker Wayne Collins held onto the ball too long before passing.

The try made amends for Walford's much-criticised performance against the Steelers two weeks ago, which almost saw coach Brian Smith drop him. "I'd rather forget my performance in the semi," Walford said, "but every bloke in Sydney has kept coming up to me and reminding me."

The low scoreline made the result hard to take, in a way a 20-point flogging wouldn't have. The Steelers were just a converted try shy of a grand final appearance. But the reason it really sticks in the craw is because of the Steelers' three disallowed tries in the second half. If just one of them was allowed – *just one* – the Steelers may have headed off to the big dance.

All three calls that still raise fans' hackles happened in the second half, with the Steelers behind on the scoreboard. The first saw the Steelers playing the ball on the Dragons 22-metre line. The ball went out to the blind side from Teitzel to Izzard, who laid on a pass for Rodwell to put the ball over the line. The cheers of Steelers fans were soon silenced when they realise McCallum has ruled Izzard's pass forward.

Rodwell lost out again through a neat left-side play where Piccinelli passed to McGregor. Losing a handle on the ball, McGregor managed to paddle the ball onto his centre partner with just his right hand. But again it was called forward.

With minutes to go, Simon found a bit of space down McIndoe's wing and put in a kick for his winger. From there it was a race between McIndoe and Walford, who had to turn and chase. The ball just rolled over the tryline and both players got there at the same time. McIndoe bounced up and did his best to sell the try, even grabbing the ball and throwing it into the air. He looked disingenuous; like he knew he hadn't scored but was trying to con the in-goal judge. But that judge wasn't having any of it – no try.

Implicit in the fans' angst is that McCallum must have surely gotten one of the calls wrong. They didn't need all of them to be stuff-ups; just one would likely give the Illawarra side enough points to win. But in taking off the scarlet-and-white glasses, the officials likely got all three calls right. McIndoe definitely knocked on rather than grounding the ball. And Rodwell's second try certainly looks suspect, thanks to that paddling of the ball by McGregor. That sort of action can see the ball go anywhere.

And the first try? Well, McCallum was right in line with the pass; a much better position than the rest of us watching old match footage on YouTube. Rodwell, who crossed the stripe twice, only to have McCallum call the play back, took a surprisingly philosophical approach to the loss. "It was disappointing that we went that close to scoring, but I don't think anyone's to blame. I think that was just the way the game went. I've wanted to play in a grand final since I was a little boy. It's just disappointing to get that close and miss out."

What gets forgotten is that the Dragons lost out too. In the first half Scott Gourley was denied a try after McCallum ruled the fingers of Tony Priddle's outstretched hands brushed the ball forward as a Noel Goldthorpe kick came down to earth. The Dragons fans have a stronger case to claim they were dudded; replays clearly show Priddle didn't touch the ball – that should have given the Saints at least an 8-0 lead. Later in the half, Neil Tierney offloaded to Jeff Hardy. The lock got into the back field with only Riolo to beat and Brad Mackay looming up in support. It's a sure try – until McCallum ruled Tierney's pass forward. Was it? Well it looked more like a legit pass than either of the Steelers forward passes. At the break, the Dragons could have been up by at least 12 points if those calls go their way.

Anyway, to focus the debate – and the blame – on the officials conveniently overlooks that the Illawarra side bombed the first chance in the game to score. Teitzel offloaded to Waddell on the Dragons 22 and he shook off tacklers Mark Coyne and Gourley, then rumbled towards the line. He broke through fullback Mick Potter's legs tackle, before Tierney managed to barely get hold of the hem of Waddell's jersey. That slowed the forward up long enough for Coyne to have another go and David Barnhill to get between him and the goal line.

Waddell ended up just two metres short of the line. From the play the ball, the Dragons goal-line defense wasn't set when the ball went right, a pass from Piccinelli finding Wishart with a clear passage to the line. He catches it, he scores. But he didn't catch it. Instead he manages to let the ball go over his shoulder and into touch.

There were other problems for the Steelers; lofted passes that went straight into touch. Not getting the ball to

McGregor early enough so he could use his step and swerve. Simon just metres from the Dragons line but not realising McCallum called six again, so he grubbered the ball away. Knock-ons. A decision to kick long straight from a scrum win on the Steelers quarter with just a minute left to go, giving up possession and the last chance for the Illawarra side to pull the game out of the fire.

Sadly, there were other reasons the Steelers lost without needing to blame the ref.

The loss made the front and back pages of the *Mercury*. On the front was a photo of Simon and Neil, heads bowed, with "tortured faces". Then the paper went on to give the referee a spray in the second paragraph. "With no help from referee Greg McCallum, the gallant Steelers fell at the last hurdle in their bid to secure a grand final berth for the first time in the club's history."

The back page photo was far more evocative. It showed Dunn and Teitzel on the bench; the former staring out onto the field with a look of disappointment – as though he could see the grand final dreams fading away – the latter with his head in his hands. Over it ran the headline "Steelers taste the agony of defeat".

In the story, Dragons fullback Potter acknowledged his side had managed to eke out a victory, despite putting just four points on the board. "I thought they had the better of it in the second half and we were lucky to get away with it."

In praising his own side's performance, Dragons coach Smith also paid tribute to the Steelers' own effort. "You coach a side to do certain things but in the end it's up to the players," he said. "They deserve all the accolades because no side is expected to defend like that for long periods against a side like Illawarra without conceding points. If any of our players had clocked off for two seconds we would have been beaten out there today."

Murray looked to salvage some positives out of the loss. "It's a marvellous achievement to get as far as we have and I just want the guys to know I'm proud of them," he said. Though he was diplomatic in discussing the referee. "As far as the decisions were concerned, I reckon he was right in disallowing the St George one – this is tongue in cheek – and I reckon we should have got our three. When you are down by four and you have a chance to throw a pass and try and win the game, I can't be dirty on anyone for that." Though you suspect Murray might have been a little dirty on the referee once the media left the sheds.

In the days after the season-ending loss, the *Mercury* looked for a bright side. The finals run had added $250,000 in gate receipts to the Steelers coffers, along with the revenue from a sudden spike in team jerseys and merchandise. Club marketing manager Ray Carney even revealed plans had been in place for a T-shirt had the Steelers qualified for the big one – which would have read "Feel the Steel".

"Wollongong went mad," Carney said about the city's response to the finals charge. "It was great; dads who had followed Manly, St George or any other number of Sydney teams suddenly found themselves supporting the Steelers because their kids were getting excited and involved. It's unified the area and done our local economy a lot of good."

Carney's comments ran in a story with the headline

"Sheilas No More", a reference to the disparaging nickname bestowed on the club by critics.

"The kids have discarded their Manly, Penrith, Canberra and company jumpers and replaced them with the scarlet and white colours of the Illawarra Steelers," the story read. "It's taken more than 10 years but the Steelers have arrived as champions in their own city. And they've done it with a team of basically local kids, with a few low-key imports for experience."

Afterword

In the autobiography of indie music legend Tex Perkins, he talks of his conflicted feelings when watching his St Kilda Saints in the 2010 grand final. The Saints' trophy cabinet was pretty sparse; there was just a 1966 grand final prize in there. It was that lack of success – and that he had moved into the suburb – that drew Perkins to the team.

"I find a culture based on struggle much more attractive than the culture of a club that's on top of the ladder and won the most premierships," he wrote.

When his team was up by five points with a few minutes to go, he had this strange feeling that a win at the MCG on grand final day would also see him lose something. Seeing the captain of his team hoisting the premiership cup in the air would also see the end of the team's culture he had grown to love.

"All that culture is going to be wiped clean if we win. Everything is going to be different. We, as St Kilda – the club and the supporters – won't be the same people anymore. I knew that everyone in and behind the club wanted this win desperately but at the same time I had this strong sense that all the things that we built our characters on would be gone. All that culture of adversity and struggle was going to be wiped clean. We'd just be another team that has won a couple of premierships."

If the Steelers had gone all the way in 1992, that would have been the club's fate too. In winning the grand final, the club and the fans would have lost a chunk of their identity that had been forged in the first 10 years of existence. They could have no longer laid claims to being the underdog against those teams from the big smoke up the road. They could no longer play with a chip on their shoulders, feeling other teams didn't really respect them.

Absolutely some fans would have been happy to make that trade; happy to experience the thrill of their side being the best in the competition. Though then the Steelers would have been just another team that had won a premiership.

Perversely, not winning the 1992 grand final – or even making it – actually served to make the culture of the Steelers stronger.

That strong 1992 season led to expectations that the Steelers were building towards something even better in the coming years, that a grand final appearance and maybe even a premiership was only a few seasons away. But it wasn't to be. For the next two seasons, it was a case of "almost good enough" for the Steelers. They finished seventh and missed the finals in 1993 even though they scored more points and let in fewer than that golden 1992 season.

Again, there were players out – McGregor missed 10 matches and McIndoe 11 – a problem when the club had lost their reliable backline replacement in Girdler. Russell only played four games all season, while Teitzel managed eight. There was also a lack of stability in the halves, with Fritz, Simon, Neil, Craig Simon, Trevor Kissell and even Riolo all getting a run in the No6 or 7. In a small highlight, big signing Bob Linder did his best – his performance in what was his final season in the competition was enough to be named Dally M second rower of the year.

What really hurt the Steelers in 1993 was being on the wrong end of some tight scorelines, 7-2 against Norths, 19-18 at Newcastle, 24-22 versus Brisbane, 9-5 against the Dragons and 4-2 to Canterbury. Turning a few of those into victories would have seen the Steelers have a very different 1993.

In 1994 they scored 166 more points than in 1992 but missed the finals by just one win. Aside from a draw against Penrith there weren't really any games they lost where the scoreline was close. It was the points they leaked which were the problem in 1994 – 128 more than the glory year of 1992.

Even when the top five became the top eight in 1995, the Steelers still struggled to make the cut. Their only finals appearance after 1992 was during the ARL-Super League mess of 1997 where there was a top seven in a 12-team comp. The Steelers finished sixth but were knocked out by the Gold Coast 25-14 in the first week of the finals. Ironically, they had thumped the Gold Coast just a week earlier to the tune of 28-6.

However, to look at later seasons with disappointment tends to diminish the spectacular achievement of the Steelers in 1992. Really, the Illawarra Steelers had no right being anywhere near the finals. They started the season wracked with injuries, losing captain Chris Walsh for the year, and the likes of McGregor, Wishart, Rodwell, Riolo, Russell and Piccinelli for extended periods.

That injury toll meant the Steelers never had the same team on the field in the same positions for two consecutive games until the finals. By any measure, that's not a recipe for a finals appearance. That's a season where a team is content to blame injuries as an excuse – and they'd have been within their rights to do that.

And yet they didn't. Instead players like Girdler, who was only expected to be a fill-in for when Origin came around, took his chance in the top grade with both hands and made it impossible for Murray to leave him out of the side. Other replacements like O'Meara, Gallagher, Pauls and Shane Wilson – players whose names are only remembered by hardcore Steelers fans – stepped up and played their part to keep the 1992 season afloat.

The injury toll stretched into the finals too; robbing them of Russell and Fritz. And yet the Steelers still finished just four measly points short of a grand final appearance. As any footy scholar will tell you, give the Steelers both of those players in the 1992 finals and you're looking at a much more successful campaign. Hell, even if you could only have one of them – I'd opt for Russell – that might be enough to swing the game.

The 1992 Steelers had it all against them. Yet they finished third and came so close to the grand final that they could smell it. If only just one of those forward passes was missed by the officials.

But here's the thing. Rather than kicking stones over the missed opportunity of a grand final, take a look back at the Steelers' 1992 season. To even get to a place where they finish one game shy of the GF is a massive accomplishment given what they had to deal with. They should have been planning their Mad Monday party a few weeks out from the last round. But they weren't. They dealt with adversity and rose above it.

That they didn't build on the success of 1992 also misses the point. Rather than focus on the negatives of the following years, put the spotlight on what should be remembered as a spectacular season.

Even if it didn't end with a premiership trophy.

Bibliography

Haddan, Steve, *The Finals*, Stephen Haddan, 2008
Headon, David, *Absolutely Bleeding Green*, Allen & Unwin, 2019
Heads, Ian, and Middleton, David, *A Centenary of Rugby League*, Pan Macmillan, 2008
Humphries, Glen, *Biff: Rugby League's Infamous Fights*, Gelding Street Press, 2022
Middleton, David, *Thirteen Years of Steel; The Story of the Illawarra Steelers*, Ironbark, 1994
Perkins, Tex, with Coupe, Stuart, *Tex*, Pan Macmillan, 2017

Alive In The Five also draws on numerous *Illawarra Mercury* articles written by the following journalists

Barry Benjamin
Julie Beun-Chown
Ben Coady
Peter Cullen
Mike Driscoll
Geoff Failes
Mike Gandon
Todd Goodwin
Nick Hartgerink
Keith Jackson
Sean Keeble
Brian Kelly
Steve Mascord

Charlie Richardson
Bill Simpson
Glenn Tobin

The website rugbyleagueproject.org was an invaluable source of information on the Steelers 1992 season.

If you liked this book why not check out some of my others? For more information visit my own micropublishing company Last Day of School, which you'll find at www.lastdayofschool.net

Glen Humphries

Jack Gibson's Fur Coat
Rugby League Artefacts and Oddities
Published by Gelding Street Press

If rugby league buried a time capsule Jack Gibson's fur coat would be the first item placed inside - if you could solve the mystery of its whereabouts. League's precious artefacts include Thurston's headgear, Langland's white boots, Reggie the Rabbit's tail and a snag from the Dragons' season-ending BBQ. Or you could fill it with stories of players who were poisoned, didn't show for the grand final or took the field drunk. In *Jack Gibson's Fur Coat*, Glen Humphries tells the stories that live on the margins. You simply couldn't make up rugby league's best yarns.

Biff
Rugby League's Infamous Fights

Published by Gelding Street Press

For close to a hundred years, the biff has been part and parcel of rugby league. And it was condoned for most of that time. As rough play like stiff arms, high tackles, spear tackles, facials and stomping were weeded out of the game, the punch remained. As recently as the 1980s league bosses would say there was nothing fans liked to see more than two forwards trading blows.

But the biff has all but disappeared in recent years, when the league finally realised there is nothing in the rule book that allows players to punch on. In *Biff*, Glen Humphries looks at some of the most infamous brawls in rugby league, from the Earl Park Riot and a match abandoned after it became a brawl to the most violent grand final and, finally, the punch that changed everything.

Glen Humphries

Friday Night at the Oxford

The story that led to reunion of legendary band Tumbleweed. An in-depth look at Sunday Painters, a band decades ahead of their time. Iconic shows like HOPE, HyFest and the Steel City Sound exhibition. These are just of the more than 100 stories about Wollongong bands and events written by journalist Glen Humphries for the *Illawarra Mercury*, from 1997 through to 2018, and his own short-lived website Dragster. The 200-plus pages of *Friday Night at the Oxford* provide a snapshot of what happened in the Wollongong music scene over the last 20-odd years – the bands, the venues, the events. It's a celebration of the music of a city.

So dig it.

Healer:
The Rise, Fall and Return of Tumbleweed

With their long hair and fuzzed-up guitars, Tumbleweed rose out of the ashes of late-80s indie band The Proton Energy Pills.

The Wollongong band hit their peak of popularity in the wake of the 1995 album *Galactaphonic*. And then proceeded to shoot themselves in the foot. Guitarist Paul Hausmeister got the sack, and then drummer Steve O'Brien left in protest. From there the band went downhill, releasing albums that met an increasingly uninterested public and playing shows in front of a half-dozen people. So it was no surprise when they called it quits in 2001.

But in 2009 they managed to heal their wounds and reunite, releasing their fifth studio album a few years later and survive the sudden death of bassplayer Jay Curley.

Journalist and music writer Glen Humphries has interviewed the members of Tumbleweed numerous times and, in Healer, takes the first complete look at the band's career.

Glen Humphries

Sounds Like an Ending: Midnight Oil, 10-1 and Red Sails in the Sunset

In 1982, Midnight Oil was a band in trouble. Their last album, *Place Without a Postcard*, was supposed to be their big breakthrough but it hadn't worked out that way. So they found themselves in London, feeling the pressure of recording what was a "make or break" album.

If this album went the same way as the last one, it could be the end of Midnight Oil. Out of the crisis came *10,9,8,7,6,5,4,3,2,1*, an album that changed everything for the band. It entered the charts and stayed there for more than three years. They started playing bigger venues – and they were able to pay back the bank manager.

Two years later, they headed to Japan to record the polarising *Red Sails in the Sunset*. It managed to do what *10-1* couldn't – give the band their first No1 album. In *Sounds Like an Ending*, journalist and author Glen Humphries takes a track-by-track look at these two albums and the times and turmoil that fuelled them.

Alright! Queen at Live Aid

On July 13, 1985, the world tuned in to watch Live Aid beamed in from Wembley in London and John F Kennedy Stadium in Philadelphia. The massive event was spawned from Bob Geldof's idea six months earlier to raise money for Ethiopian famine victims through the release of the charity single, *Do They Know It's Christmas?*.

The iconic performance on that day came from Queen, a band that had been considering calling it quits just months earlier. Performing in front of an estimated audience of 1.9 billion people, the fourpiece stole the show and revitalised their career.

Alright takes a look back at Queen's performance on that day as well as revisiting the origins of the Band Aid single and the logistics behind getting Live Aid off the ground.

Little Darling
Daryl Braithwaite and The Horses

Most musicians only get one chance at fame. Daryl Braithwaite has managed to have three of them. He joined a band called Sherbet in 1970 and, a year later, they had their first hit - and there were an astonishing 19 more to come.

But Sherbet's fans grew up and moved on so the band folded in the early 1980s. At the end of that decade, Braithwaite found himself with a surprise hit album in *Edge*. He followed it up a few years later with *Rise* - the album that included a little tune called *The Horses*. That song went to No1, but a lawsuit and diminishing sales saw him pushed out of the limelight.

Then, in the early 2000s, something strange happened – kids at gigs started singing *The Horses* back at Braithwaite. Soon enough, this song that might have otherwise faded away galloped back and became an Australian anthem. *Little Darling* looks at the unusual phenomenon of *The Horses* and offers up an explanation for how it happened.

The Slab: 24 Stories of Beer in Australia

Beer. You know it and, chances are, you love it. But you might not know the part beer has played in Australian history. Right from the start beer was there. It was on board The Endeavour when Captain Cook set sail for Australia. It was drunk not long after the First Fleet landed in Botany Bay.

It was there when World War I soldiers got a skinful and ran riot in the streets of Sydney. It was there during the era of six o'clock closing where people were still drinking it long after the little hand had passed the six. It was even there when it really shouldn't have been - when Canberra declared itself an alcohol-free zone.

"History as it should be written. With beer. About beer. Crisp. Refreshing. Won't cause bloat."
John Birmingham, author of Leviathan

Glen Humphries

James Squire: The Biography

After getting caught swiping a few chickens from a neighbour, James Squire was sentenced to seven years in Sydney Cove. You could say it was the best thing he ever did – it led to him become a brewer, policeman, property tycoon, respected citizen and a bloody rich guy. But if all you know about James Squire is what you've read on labels on beer bottles, then you really don't know that much at all.

This book – the first biography of Squire – separates the facts from the well-known myths. Along the way you'll also discover a few other things about Sydney Cove, including Captain Arthur Phillip's efforts to get his hands on some Aboriginal heads for a friend, the early Australian fondness for cider rather than beer, the fight rival brewer John Boston had over a dead pig and the marine who tried to trade his hat for an Aboriginal child.

Night Terrors: The True Story of the Kingsgrove Slasher

Between 1956 and 1959, suburban Sydney was terrorised by a phantom known as the Kingsgrove Slasher. A peeping Tom, he graduated to breaking into houses to watch people sleep before later slashing women and girls with a razor while they lay in their beds.

He punched a 21-year-old woman into unconsciousness, breaking her teeth and cutting her mouth, hit a teenage girl in the face with a piece of wood and slashed a deep wound across the stomach of a 64-year-old woman. The Slasher also groped teens in their beds, and one of his 18 victims was just seven years old.

Night Terrors is the first detailed account of the Kingsgrove Slasher case. It draws on hundreds of newspaper articles written at the time - which show the level of fear in the community - as well as the transcripts from the court hearings, which had been sealed since 1959.

EBOOKS
The Six-Pack: Stories from the World of Beer

From stories of monks making beer, to rumours of an unpleasant secret "ingredient" in a world-famous drink, there are plenty of great stories about beer. And six of them are captured in this ebook.

Beer is Fun!

Oh look, it's the best moments from Beer is Your Friend, the blog that won a national beer writing award and also inspired Dale to leave a comment "give ur self an uppercut u oxygen thief".

Why should you buy this book? Because it's 300-plus and it'll cost you just a few measly bucks. What else in life will give you loads of entertainment for such a low price? Go on, buy it. If you don't like it, I'll give you your money back. Well, that's a lie, I won't give you a cent.

www.ingramcontent.com/pod-product-compliance
Lightning Source LLC
Chambersburg PA
CBHW062047290426
44109CB00027B/2756